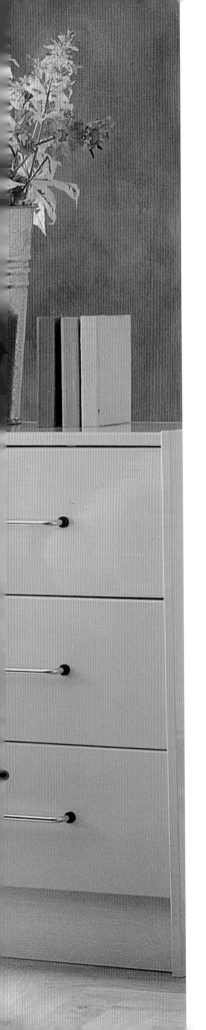

REVAMP YOUR
FURNITURE

Liz Wagstaff

with Mark Thurgood

Special photography by Debbie Patterson

Quadrille Publishing

For Jean and Denis
for their unfailing help and support throughout this book

p. 1: *Crackle glaze and a hand-stamped blind on wardrobe shelving (pp. 60–3)*

pp. 2–3: *High-gloss lacquer on a set of drawers (pp. 56–7)*

p. 4: *Stencilled fruit on loom chairs (pp. 106–9)*

p. 5: *Gilded chequering on a circular table (pp. 75–7)*

Art Director: Mary Evans

Project Editor: Mary Davies

Art Editor: Rachel Gibson

Studio Photography: Nicki Dowey

Picture Researcher: Helen Fickling

Production Manager: Candida Lane

This edition first published in 2007 by Quadrille Publishing

Copyright © Text 1998 Liz Wagstaff
Copyright © Design and layout 1998 Quadrille Publishing Limited

ISBN-13: 978 184400 5222

Printed and bound in Spain

CONTENTS

INTRODUCTION

The purpose of this book is to explore ways of turning cast-off and budget-range furniture into functional pieces uniquely styled to suit your living spaces. Our aim is to provide you with a bank of inspirational ideas and technical advice on how to achieve custom-built results easily and cheaply.

How often have you scoured furniture stores and not found quite what you were looking for? Maybe the size or shape was wrong. Maybe the style or color didn't complement your decor. Or maybe that wonderful character piece you discovered bore a ridiculous price tag.

As designers, we have strong views on what we want the furniture around us to look like and what we want it to do. Often making over other pieces, new or old, is the only affordable way to achieve both. For more years than I care to admit, we had in one of our rooms at home a bulky, Gothic-style bed snapped up very cheaply in a weak moment at a furniture sale. When the old dinosaur finally became too much to bear, we chopped away the bulk of the head- and foot-boards, gilded it silver, using aluminum leaf, and dressed it in pale, floaty cotton for a soft, antique French look—a magical transformation and it cost us very little. So don't regard making over as a last resort. In the current shift toward simplicity in natural, uncluttered, or minimal interiors for busy people living on tight budgets, there is plenty of scope for painted and adapted furniture which exactly meets your needs with a personalized look that store-bought furniture simply cannot have. The secret is to dream the dream and then have the confidence to go ahead and make it real.

We find inspiration everywhere—in art and pattern books, in magazines, new and old, in visits to great houses and museums, even in jaunts to the movies. I'm one of those irritating people likely to come out humming the set. There is a long history to draw upon since men and women began demanding more of their furniture than

Left: Heavily aged paint in a country setting: too extreme for all but the most romantic taste, it is a perfect demonstration of how and where paint breaks down on a much-used piece. To simulate the tones, I would try a base coat of ocher under top coats of aqua, gray, and somber green, separated by three wax-resist treatments (see page 144), and a lot of hard rubbing back.

Below: This pretty cabinet is more softly aged. A darker glaze (see page 147) could dull down the appealing two-color scheme, and the swept top might be cut from MDF with strips of beading above and below the door.

Bright daubed paint and a pair of thick cord handles lift a sturdy cabinet above the ordinary. This surprisingly harmonious effect is achieved by loosely following the order of the colors of the spectrum. To duplicate, use artists' acrylic colors. For a less expensive alternative, you could try just two sections of the spectrum.

pure function—if, indeed, there was ever any distinction between function and form. I reckon that the world's first chair made some statement about the person who chose to live with it.

Your adaptations and paint and decorative finishes can be "authentic" or high fantastical, grand or simple, even primitive. Until relatively recently in many parts of the world—in Poland, in Mexico, and in the Indian subcontinent, for example—there have been vigorous and inspiring folk traditions of hand-painted furniture.

In our experience there are two important maxims to bear in mind in the search for suitable pieces to make over. One: almost any surface can be prepared for painting, so don't despair when confronted with plastic laminate. With a little imagination that seventies kitchen cabinet could turn country sophisticate or space-age futuristic. And two: style, even shape, isn't immutable. A little adaptation can create any number of new looks to fit Granny's china cupboard for life in the fast lane.

The very first step is to look at what you already have—the fixtures you acquired when you moved in, the cabinet you bought but never cared for, the table that no longer suits your taste or fills a space. Then, when friends or family offer you their rejects, look twice before you say no or hide them in the attic. Moving can be a wonderful opportunity if you keep your mind open. What does it matter if someone's dump fest brings you a fifties chair crying out for retro découpage?

Just one word of warning before you widen the hunt: no matter how much some carved oak armoire that's been in the family for decades seems to yearn for paint, think first. Genuine antiques and good furniture demand respect. We are not in the business of restoration, so our house rule is simple. If the piece is sound and the style and wood are good, leave it for someone who will love it for itself. And if that turns out to be you, get expert advice for restoration.

The next place to look is the secondhand shops. Get to know those in your area. Do they specialize in certain kinds of stock? Which day of

Left: This almost monumental adaptation is a wonderful example of the way in which a basic shape can be built up layer by layer using standard panels and moldings from home centers. It is decorated with silver paint or metal leaf and finished with an aging glaze (see pages 35 and 168).

Right: There's a confident color sense and an eye for the potential in scrap material at work in these two makeovers with an ethnic feel. The wooden screen has been découpaged (see page 160) with masses of intricate Indian cards, wrap, and advertising. The simple chair is bound with strips of fabric, glued in place. I love the occasional buttons sewn on arms and legs.

Transformation time for some boring, but sound laminate kitchen units (see page 89): masking techniques and spray paints have created a tough surface, and new knobs and handles add the finishing touches.

the week does the new stock arrive? You need to be first on the doorstep to claim the pick of the crop. Chat to the proprietors and give them an idea of the kind of things you might be interested in. As you do your research, study prices. Whose are higher than average? Whose are low? Resist the temptation to snap up the first piece that matches your brief—it's galling to find a similar item down the street at half the price. But remember: market forces operate in this world, too. If the look you want is trendy, you'll be hard pressed to find a bargain.

Local papers are another good hunting ground. Here you will find the dates of local auctions and a classified ads section for unwanted items. If you are able to put in the time and can find suitable transportation, this is the place to get a great bargain, simply by cutting out the middleman. Garage sales offer the same incentive.

The other place to look is in the large retail outlets that produce budget ranges of new softwood and wood-based furniture. Their often basic shapes are an excellent starting point for adaptation and decoration, and, because some are sold unfinished, protected with just a thin coat of sealant, preparation is cut to the minimum—always a plus.

Making over old and new furniture is a great way to put a personal stamp on your surroundings. It can be a solitary pleasure or a companionable way to spend time with a partner or friend. With this book beside you, you have access to an almost unlimited range of possibilities. Enjoy.

PART ONE

PREPARATION

A guide to the tools, equipment, and materials used to adapt and decorate furniture, plus detailed advice on preparing the surface and some of the techniques of simple adaptation

This kitchen-of-the-future suggests two interesting makeovers. First: the wavy table edge. Extra-thin plywood, cut to shape with a jigsaw and glued into place would be a good base for the mosaic. Note the repeat shape on the back of the unit, where a stouter, non-flexible material could be used. (Mosaic tiles seem to have been teamed with the opaque, colored glass lozenges found in florists and specialist candle shops.) Second: the plain zinc inserts on the doors. For safety's sake, ignore the stove on casters and the part-tiled floor.

CLEANING
AND PREPARATION

You know it's true. Thorough cleaning and surface preparation are an essential part of any successful paint or decorative transformation, so we make no apology for devoting the first six pages to what may seem an unexciting subject. The chart on pages 16–17 guides you through the treatment of most of the materials you are likely to encounter as you reclaim and adapt old and budget-range furniture.

At the risk of putting you off before you've begun, we must caution you that junk furniture will more often than not be dirty, even greasy, when you find it. It makes sense to do the first cleaning stage outdoors if you can, and those of a nervous disposition should bribe someone else to make a first foray with a stiff wire brush.

Most of the materials and equipment you need are very familiar, even household objects—some you may have already. Others, such as protective masks and goggles, are perhaps less obvious but important. Don't allow some long-experienced do-it-yourselfer to persuade you otherwise. Before buying any protective equipment, read the label to make sure it is adequate for the job you are doing.

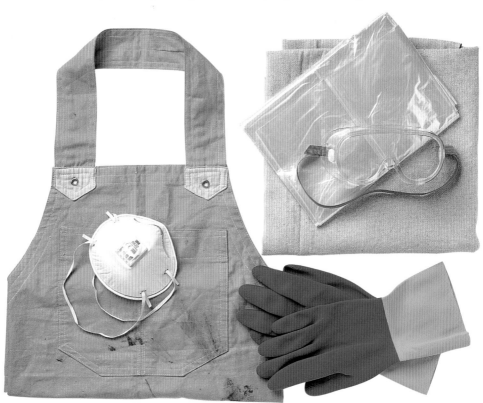

PROTECTION Preparing surfaces can be messy, even hazardous work, so don't forget to protect youself and your home. Cotton aprons or overalls and rubber gloves are great for most undertakings. Masks help cut down the risk of inhaling dust as you rub down (see also page 18) and protect against harmful vapors, but you need stout plastic goggles, too. Cotton and plastic drop cloths come in various sizes. But beware: liquids can "pool" on plastic.

CLEANING AND RUBBING DOWN

Dust cloths, a plastic dishwashing bowl, synthetic sponge, and scourer should all be part of your basic kit. Never throw cotton shirts or sheets away. Tear and store —they make wonderful lint-free rags. De-greaser solution is best for cleaning greasy surfaces, though you can substitute detergent. Several rinses with clean water are essential.

Steel wool cleans and provides a tooth for paint on metal and plastics; use with mineral spirit (top right). Buy loose in small bales or try the synthetic pad form. Sandpaper needs little introduction. Fine and medium grades are the two you are likely to need, but both clog quickly, must be used dry, and create dust, so don't use them if you think the paint is lead based. Gloss paint is now lead-free, but be wary of old painted furniture. The gray abrasive papers shown here are used wet and do not cause dust.

Chemical paint strippers are the best way to remove paint or varnish, and denatured alcohol will clean metals such as zinc or tin.

SIMPLE REPAIRS

Don't take on any piece that is structurally unsound—it is not worth spending time and money on something that may not in the end be able to perform as well as you hoped. Minor surface damage can be repaired (see pages 16–17 for specific advice) or may even enhance some of the aging techniques in Part Three; and, as the project illustrated on page 67 makes clear, a wrecked door need not defeat you. Once wood-based surfaces are thoroughly clean and before repairing, check carefully for woodworm. If you find any suspect holes —they are round and approx. $1/16$in. (2mm.) in diameter—brush all surfaces twice with a woodworm killer and inject into all holes.

FILLING HOLES AND CRACKS

Wood and wood-based material

Apply flexible, ready-mixed filler with a filling knife, spreading downward from the top. Overfill, removing any obvious excess quickly and smoothing to make sanding easier.

Laminate

Using car-body filler and a spatula, fill damaged sections by spreading downward and then smoothing with a horizontal stroke. This dual action consolidates and flattens for sanding.

SECURING RAISED LAMINATE

1 Apply wood glue liberally to the base to which the laminate is to be attached, making sure the surface is completely covered.

Note To secure a new sheet of laminate to a surface, use contact cement (see page 27).

2 Position appropriate pieces of batten and one or more C-clamps to ensure that the whole section is kept completely flat while it dries. Use a rag to wipe off excess glue before drying begins, taking care not to disturb the clamp.

MENDING A WOBBLY CHAIR LEG

Find the point of weakness—it is sure to be a corner joint—and drill four pilot holes, two in each visible, outer side of the upright. They must be positioned in alternate planes so that the countersunk screws will pass through the upright into the adjacent side of the seat base. Insert and tighten the screws to secure. Smooth wood filler over the screw heads to conceal. **Note** For clarity, only two screws are shown.

REMOVING OLD NAILS

Nail with no head

If pliers are no use, place a thin piece of wood beside the nail to protect the surface and create purchase. Bend with a claw hammer as shown and then pull and twist until released.

Nail with a head

Grasp the head of the nail with a claw hammer, again protecting the surface with a thin piece of wood, and lever it out by firmly rocking the tool forward from claw to hammer head.

REPLACING DAMAGED HINGES

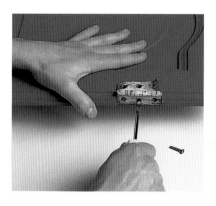

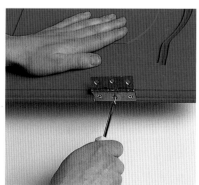

1 Take care not to damage the wood as you unscrew. Throw away screws as well as hinges.
2 Screw in the new hinges, using the old holes. Screwheads must lie flush or the door will bind.

To correct, buy screws one gauge smaller. If the screws do not fit firmly, pad the holes with tiny dowels. For a stronger hinge, choose a longer one; but beware—it will be wider too.

PREPARING THE SURFACE

All the standard surfaces are listed below. Seek expert advice from a local hardware store if you cannot find the one you want. Dip-stripping is not an option for large pieces of furniture: it may cause warping or loose joints. Untreated live knots in new wood will create dark patches in paint over time, so apply shellac before you paint. Treating knots that are oozing resin is a long process; avoid it if you can.

SURFACE	CLEAN/ DEGREASE	REPAIR/ FILL	RUB DOWN/SAND after repair and/or construction	PRIMER/ UNDERCOAT
WOOD **Painted** water- or oil-based **Sealed** with PVA adhesive **Waxed**	Wash with mild dish-soap solution, using lint-free rag or tac cloth, and leave to dry.	Fill holes with fine-grade flexible wood filler.	**Sound surfaces** Flat latex/sealed/ waxed: use fine-grit sandpaper to provide surface for painting. Gloss/enamel paint: use wet-and-dry paper for surface preparation. **Unsound surfaces** Take off flaky or rough paint with a scraper; for obstinate areas, use a chemical gel or paste paint stripper.	**Waxed surfaces** Rub a thin film of dry soap all over the surface and then treat as appropriate (see below). **Sound surfaces** Unnecessary **Bare patches** Spot-prime with appropriate material: • acrylic wood primer (w) Allow to dry (2 hours). • oil-based u/coat (o) Allow to dry (16 hours).
Varnished	Brush well with stiff-bristled brush and then wash as above.	See above.	**Sound surfaces** See latex/sealed/ waxed above. **Unsound surfaces** See Unsound surfaces above. Alternative: varnish remover.	See Sound surfaces and Bare patches above.
Unpainted	Wipe with damp, lint-free rag. Do not soak: water will raise grain and may cause wood to warp.	See above. Alternative: all-purpose filler. **New wood** Apply shellac to prevent knot seepage.	Use fine-grit sandpaper to provide surface for painting.	Prime with appropriate material: • acrylic wood primer (w) • oil-based u/coat (o) See above for drying times.
MDF **Painted**	See Wood, painted.	Fill holes with fine-grade flexible wood filler or all-purpose filler.	See above.	**Sound surfaces** Unnecessary **Bare patches** See below.
Unpainted	See Wood, unpainted.	See above.	Use fine-grit sandpaper to provide surface for painting. Be gentle: MDF cannot be made smoother by sanding.	Prime with appropriate material: • acrylic wood primer (w) • latex paint (w) • oil-based u/coat (o) Latex paint drying time: 2–3 hours.
PLYWOOD **Painted**	See Wood, painted.	See above.	Use fine-grit sandpaper to provide surface for painting.	See MDF, painted.

• Clean again after rubbing down/sanding. Use warm soapy water and a lint-free rag or tac cloth.
• Use a dust mask if sanding, rubber gloves if using denatured alcohol or paint strippers. Good ventilation is vital at all times.

SURFACE	CLEAN/ DE-GREASE	REPAIR/ FILL	RUB DOWN/SAND after repair and/or construction	PRIMER/ UNDERCOAT
PLYWOOD **Varnished**	See Wood, varnished.	See MDF, painted.	See Plywood, painted.	See Wood, painted (Sound surfaces and Bare patches).
Unpainted	See Wood, unpainted.	See above.	See above.	See Wood, unpainted.
PARTICLEBOARD **Wood veneered** (inc. ash, pine, mahogany, teak)	See Wood, as appropriate.	See above.	See above.	See Wood, as appropriate.
Melamine-coated (white, black, wood effect)	Wash with de-greaser solution, using lint-free rag, and leave to dry.	See above.	See above.	See Wood, unpainted.
MASONITE **Painted**	See MDF, painted.	See MDF, painted.	See MDF, painted.	See MDF, painted.
LAMINATES AND PLASTICS (inc. wood effects on particleboard, Masonite, plywood)	Wash with de-greaser solution or wipe clean with mineral spirit, using steel wool, and leave to dry.	Fill cracks and holes with car-body filler.	Use abrasive paper to provide tooth for painting.	See Wood, unpainted.
FERROUS METAL (e.g. iron and steel) **Bare**	Wipe with mineral spirit, using steel wool, and leave to dry. **Heavy rust** Rub down with wire brush, then clean as above.	See above.	See above.	Prime with either: • metal primer (o) Allow to dry (12 hours). • red oxide primer (o) Allow to dry (16 hours). Follow with universal acrylic primer if using water-based paint.
Lacquered, painted, or plastic-coated	**Sound** Wash with de-greaser solution and leave to dry. **Unsound** Use a chemical stripper to remove the covering.	See above.	See above.	**Sound surfaces** Unnecessary **Bare patches** Spot "prime" as above.
NON-FERROUS METAL (e.g. aluminum, chrome plating, tin, and zinc)	Wipe with mineral spirit or denatured alcohol, using steel wool, wash with detergent, and leave to dry.	See above.	See above.	Prime with: • metal primer (o) Allow to dry (12 hours). Follow with universal acrylic primer if using water-based paint.
RATTAN, RUSH, WILLOW, AND OTHER BASKET WEAVE	Wash with de-greaser solution, using lint-free rag, and leave to dry fully. Do not soak.	Seek expert advice.	**Rush (sealed or painted)** Use very fine steel wool very gently to provide tooth for painting. **Rattan and Willow (sealed or painted)** See Rush. Or use very fine sandpaper very gently. **Unsealed and unpainted** Unnecessary	**New surfaces** Unnecessary **Painted surfaces** Prime with either: • acrylic spray primer (w) • acrylic wood primer (w) Apply with brush to heavily painted surfaces.

- Clean again after rubbing down/sanding. Use warm, soapy water and lint-free rag.
- Use a mask if sanding, rubber gloves if working with mineral spirit or paint strippers. Good ventilation is vital at all times.

(w) = water-based (o) = oil-based   Water-based primers/undercoats for water-based finishes; oil-based primers/undercoats for oil-based finishes

MATERIALS

Good lumberyards and home centers will hold all the stock you need and can give valuable advice. We have incorporated some of the commonest materials into our adaptations, but it is well worthwhile looking around to see what else is available. Stores reflect changing tastes and trends, and browsing will spark all sorts of ideas.

The wood and wood-based boards we list are available in various thicknesses. The sizes we suggest were chosen to suit both the function and look we wanted for a specific piece of furniture. You must judge what will suit yours. We favor MDF, or medium-density fiberboard, above plywood for most adaptations on painted furniture. It can be shaped so easily with a jigsaw without splintering, and its ultra-smooth surface is a delight to paint or stain. Composed of wood fibers bonded with synthetic resins, wax, and formaldehyde, it produces a fine dust when worked, so, as with all solid timber and wood-based materials, you must take precautions when cutting or drilling (see the chart opposite). Fortunately sanding only makes it rougher, not smoother, which cuts preparation time.

MDF (left) AND PLYWOOD
MDF's smooth face and profile create the better surface for paint. Plywood may contain three or more layers and be of different thicknesses. Unlike MDF, plywood can simply be varnished.

WORKING WITH WOOD AND WOOD-BASED MATERIALS

Wear protective clothing
- Goggles
- Disposable face mask
- Gloves and long sleeves for those with sensitive skin

Work outside or in a well-ventilated area
- Cover carpets and furniture with drop cloths
- Avoid sources of heat or ignition

Dispose of waste in sealed plastic bags
- Dampen dust with fine spray
- Sweep carefully
- Vacuum

A disposable face mask

BATTENS
Made of softwood, standard batten is square or rectangular and is available in a range of sizes. It has many uses, including edging on wood-based material and support for shelves or when fitting extra pieces of wood. Quarter-round wood is used to cover joins and retain glass.

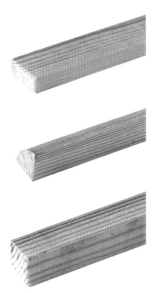

DOWEL ROD
Useful for drapery poles and (see page 130) bed posts, hardwood dowel rod is widely available in various diameters from ¼ to 1in. (6mm.–25mm.). Softwood versions can be found in some larger sizes. Short sections of the smallest sizes are used to plug worn screw holes (see page 15).

KNOW YOUR WOOD

SOFTWOOD	HARDWOOD
From coniferous trees Pine, Fir, Spruce	**From broad-leaved trees** Beech, Mahogany, Maple, Oak, Teak
Description • More easily dented—paint and varnish increase resistance • Unpainted wood darkens quickly in direct sunlight • Widely available in many sizes	**Description** • Stronger—more resistant to damage and carries heavier loads without bending • Widely available in various sizes
Handling characteristics • Easy to smooth by sanding • Live knots must be treated before painting (see page 16) • Easy to glue, screw into, or nail; use bradawl for pilot holes • Easy to stain or varnish	**Handling characteristics** • Easy to glue • Harder to screw into—drill for pilot holes • Avoid nailing (danger of splits); drill pilot holes if essential • Responds well to stain or polish

EDGE TRIMS
Decorative fretwork is available in a wide variety of styles and is usually sold by the foot. Lumberyards will stock a range, but for a wider selection approach the specialist mail-order companies. Fretwork is easy to cut to length with a backsaw and can be used to trim shelves, doors, and simple cabinets. You can finish it with latex flat, oil, or any other paint.

MOLDINGS
Obtainable in a variety of styles and designs, some moldings can be used as another form of edge trim or for adding panels to flush doors. Others can be combined to reshape a piece completely (see page 8). Sold by the foot, they are available in hard and softwood from lumberyards, home centers, and framing suppliers. The hardwood versions will be more expensive, so if you have a choice, don't buy them when you plan to paint.

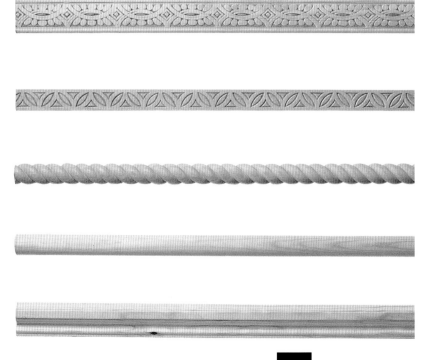

METAL: SHEET, MESH, AND WIRE Gardeners will be familiar with chicken wire, but it also makes a cheap mesh for use indoors if sprayed with metallic paint. Good home centers will carry a variety of decorative meshes and wires for the same purpose. Chicken wire is usually sold in rolls, meshes by the sheet. The zinc and tin plate used to cover surfaces and for punched-tin effects are also often sold by the sheet. You can reduce the sheen (see darker sample) by rubbing with steel wool, used alone or with mineral spirit.

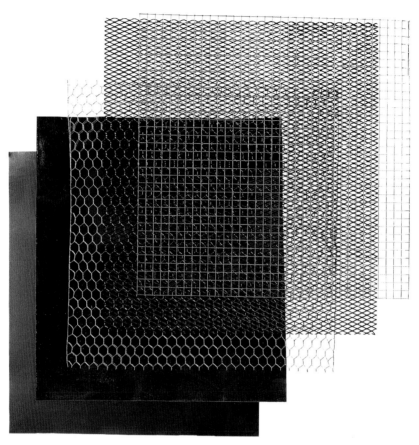

APPLYING CHROME TRIM OR FAKE LEADING

1 Peeling off a little of the backing at a time, press the self-adhesive strip firmly onto the smooth edge. Continue in this way, holding the trim in one hand and pressing with the other, until the piece has been positioned or until you need to cut to fit.

2 Cut (if required) with scissors and press into place. Use the rounded handle of a knife or fork (sometimes, as here, a tool is provided) to smooth gently along its length, removing any bumps. Two or more strips may be required to cover the edge.

CUTTING WOOD

WOODCUTTING KIT
A backsaw for accurate cutting and ease of use; a chisel to pare away slivers of wood; a small wooden or plastic miter box for accurate cutting of batten, dowel, and molding; an electric-powered jigsaw and selection of blades for cutting and shaping wood and metal; a selection of C-clamps for securing wood while cutting or gluing

Experienced do-it-yourselfers may find little that is new in this and some of the following sections, which are designed very largely to encourage those less familiar with the equipment and techniques associated with adapting old and budget furniture. But don't skip them entirely—there may be something here for you.

All but the most practically challenged probably own a saw. If you don't, a hand saw is not a major expense. Jigsaws are more expensive, but they certainly make long cuts on MDF and plywood much easier and once you are confident, they are a dream if you want to create decorative shapes quickly and easily. They can be rented at a daily rate from tool-rental stores, and if you are not sure how you will make out, it is sensible to "test drive" one for a day. If you don't have the luxury of a permanent workbench, you might like to invest in an adjustable one. These are available at all good home centers, and even the most basic provides a stable surface to which you can clamp materials for cutting or drilling. However, it is best to lay large sheets on the floor, supported on battens arranged in the direction of the cut but out of reach. Make sure there is nothing underneath that might be damaged.

WORKING WITH HAND AND POWER SAWS

See the safety chart on page 19, and that for working with power tools (if appropriate) on page 29. Never work in a cramped area, especially when using a jigsaw, and make sure the light is good. If you plan to use a jigsaw, ask people not to disturb you—any surprise is dangerous. Tuck all wires and cables out of the way. Make sure that tools are in working order and that clamps, if used, are firmly tightened. Before cutting, use a straight-edged piece of paper to confirm that the ends of moldings, dowels, and battens are true, and double-check measurements.

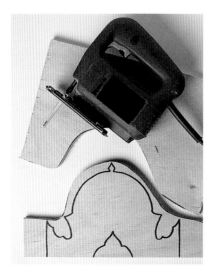

Cutting out detailed shapes

Begin by cutting away the excess material in a series of simple cuts. Then cut out the detail. This also applies to working with a coping saw —the hand tool used for shaping wood.

Cutting out accurately

Use a soft pencil to mark the cutting line clearly, and cut on the waste side of it. If you cut on the pencil line, the piece will be a little shorter than you intended.

Using a backsaw

The short, straight, rectangular blade makes this an easier saw to control than the longer, more flexible crosscut saw, and it also cuts through plywood and thin board more easily. It is for these reasons that we recommend it to the beginner who needs to buy a hand saw. To begin a cut, grip the saw firmly, extending your first finger along the side of the handle, place the saw at the forward edge of the marked line (see left and above), and draw it back toward you a couple of times to ease the teeth into a better position before you begin to saw.

USING METAL

Inexpensive metal detail has been used for many centuries to add character and charm to simple furniture and smaller decorative objects, so there's much to learn from the folk cultures of Asia, Europe, and the Americas. But it's probably retro chic and specifically the utility look of the fifties diner that has prompted the current craze for metal-covered worktops. The tools you need for our metal-based techniques—fitting wire inserts, punching tin, and covering surfaces—are all widely available, inexpensive, and easy to use. For information on materials, see pages 21 and 40 and the adhesives chart on page 27.

METALWORKING Masking and gaffer tape to cover sharp edges and position designs; a hand-held staple gun to secure chicken wire (and fabric); cotton gloves to prevent grease buildup; a tile cutter (center) to score surfaces; a center punch (below) plus hammer to punch tin; a brick chisel to define creases in zinc (see opposite); heavy-duty tinsnips to cut sheet metal; a small hacksaw to cut metal rod; a rubber mallet to flatten cut edges

SHAPING AND BENDING A ZINC SHEET

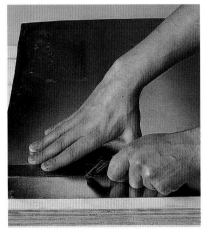

1 Zinc needs a little persuasion to bend cleanly and accurately. For more about the technique of covering a work surface, see the French Dresser project on pages 73–4 (Preparing the zinc and Fixing the zinc). Once any necessary cuts have been made to aid folding and all the edges have been tapped with a rubber mallet to flatten, position a metal ruler along each fold line in turn while you score the metal lightly with a tile cutter. Practice the technique on a piece of scrap first—too much pressure and you may cut too far through the metal.

2 Grasping the brick chisel by its shaft, place its tip on one of the scored lines and tap the other end with the hammer. Reposition the chisel, repeating to improve the crease along the whole line. Repeat on all fold lines.

3 Position the zinc on the surface, right side up. Using a batten approx. 12in. (30cm.) long as a cushion between hammer and metal, tap along the edges of the surface to bend the zinc down as you create the first fold on each side.

WORKING WITH METAL

- Always wear goggles.
- Cover raw edges of tin or zinc with masking tape to avoid cuts.
- Never fully close tinsnips when cutting metal.
- Wear heavy-duty gardening gloves when cutting chicken wire.
- Use pliers to bend cut ends of chicken wire inward to prevent grazes.
- Place a tab of masking tape at drilling point to prevent bit from slipping.
- Make pilot hole with center punch and hammer before drilling through or into metal.
- Sand or file exposed cut edges on finished work to smooth.

JOINING 1

Screws are conventionally measured by length and by the diameter or gauge of the upper, unthreaded section (or shank). The longer or wider a screw is, the greater its fixing strength. Most of the screws we use in our projects are gauge 6 or 8. The screw most commonly used today, which we recommend for all practical purposes, is the flat-head wood screw, available with a plain, single slot; with crossed slots (Phillips and, in some countries, the similar Pozidrive); and with a square, "torque," slot. Flat-head screws are designed to be countersunk, so that they lie flush, so you need a drill bit or hand tool to bore space for the head. You also need a screwdriver to match the type of screw. Finishing nails are the only practical nails we use here; the copper roofing nails must be trimmed with a single oblique cut to fit.

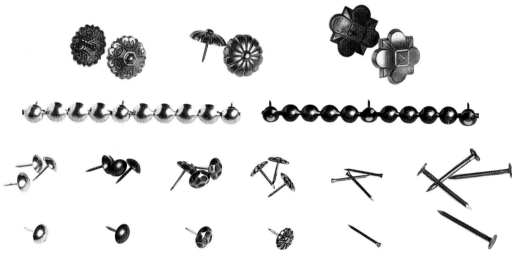

DECORATIVE NAILS
Large studs, found in good hardware or specialist restoration stores; stud

trim, a useful way to reduce time spent tacking—available from upholsterers; range of upholstery

studs, available in home centers; copper roofing nails (far right) look good in zinc; finishing

nails (second from right), not strictly decorative, but used to secure trim and molding

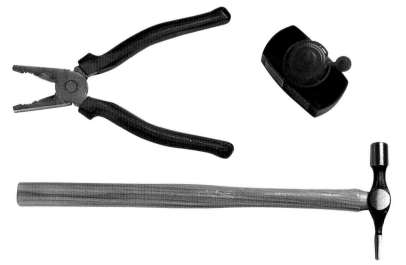

JOINING TOOLS 1
A light tack hammer is ideal for our adaptations. The narrow section opposite the head, called a flat peen, is used for starting off finishing nails held between the fingers. Invest in a good pair of pliers —you can use them to trim nails that are too long. Brush wood glue onto battens and moldings before inserting nails.

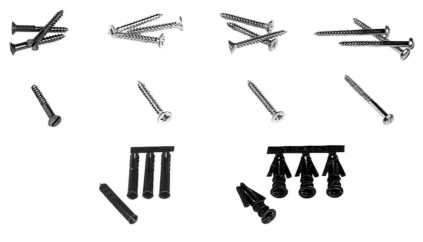

SCREWS AND WALL FASTENERS Three types of flat-head screw: (from left) single slot; Phillips cross head; Pozidrive cross head. The brass dome heads are decorative. Wall fasteners: (far left) anchors for masonry; expanding hollow wall fastener

| Single-slot head | Pozidrive head | Phillips head |

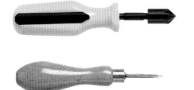

JOINING TOOLS 2 A spirit level for checking alignment; a screwdriver—you can buy both single and ratchet types for interchangeable heads; a counter-sinking tool to prepare headroom for flat-head screws; a bradawl to make small holes in softwood and metal

WHICH ADHESIVE?

JOIN	TO			ADHESIVE TYPE
	WOOD-BASED MATERIALS inc. laminates	PLASTICS inc. laminates	METALS	
Ceramic	✓	✓	✓	**Ceramic tile adhesive** Thick paste dries white. Also use for beads & shells. Alternative: **Clear, strong PVA glue**
Fabric	✓	✓	✓	**Fabric glue** See also White glue.
Metal	✓	✓	✓	**Contact cement** Applied to both surfaces. Dries clear.
Paper	✓	✓	✓	**White glue** Dries clear. Dilute with water to stiffen fabric for decorative detail (see page 116). See also Spray adhesive.
Plant material	✓	✓	✕	**Spray adhesive** Available in different strengths. Temporary bonding for masking with leaves or cut paper.
Plastic	✓	✓	✕	New laminate: As Metal. Repair: As wood, light duty (no pins).
Wood	✓	✓	✕	Light duty: **Wood glue plus finishing nails** Dries clear Heavy duty: **Quick-dry epoxy glue** Two-part mix dries clear.

The tiny head of a finishing nail is almost invisible when hammered firmly into position. If you want to conceal it completely, you can use a small center punch to drive it below the surface and fill the hole with flexible wood filler, but that's probably unnecessary for all practical purposes if you plan to paint. Nail the thinner material to the thicker, and, for strength, where possible choose a nail at least twice as long as the thickness of the piece to be secured. When nailing thin pieces or near the end of wood, blunt the nail with a hammer to prevent splits, and bore a small pilot hole with a bradawl.

When using screws, again choose one at least twice as long as the piece to be secured. To screw one piece of wood to another, you need two pilot holes for ease of entry. They should be narrower and (in total) shorter than the screw, so that the thread has something to bite on. First mark the screw position with a pencil cross on the piece to be secured, and drill a hole through it, using an appropriate bit. This is the time to use a countersink bit or tool, if required, checking the depth with the screw. Position the two pieces with the drilled section on top, and mark the lower pilot hole by pushing a bradawl or pencil through the hole. Remove the upper piece and drill the second hole. Realign the two pieces, insert the screw, and use a hand or powered driver to secure.

Get advice when fixing to walls. Tapping will determine whether it's a solid or hollow surface, but you must choose between a range of hollow wall fasteners which spread the load. Brass screws are softer than steel ones, so prepare the thread by screwing in and removing a steel screw of the same size first to reduce the risk of damaging the head.

POWER DRILL
Powered drills and drill/drivers can speed many joining jobs. Shown here is a standard drill and selection of drill bits for working in wood and metal. Also shown is the chuck key, which is required on this model to change the bits. Some have a built-in component for easier changing of bits. A variety of drills and drill/drivers is available. Check the bits included; separate sets are also available.

WORKING WITH HAND AND POWER DRILLS

Make sure work is securely clamped to a stable surface. Insert a piece of wood between the clamp and work to prevent damage to the surface. You could rent or buy a drill stand to ensure that the holes you drill are straight, but there are cheaper solutions. Keep the drill at chest height. Hold it parallel to your body when drilling downward, onto a workbench. Hold it at a right angle to your body when drilling a hole in front of you, as into a wall. Standing a try square on end by the drill also helps. To drill to an exact depth, place tape on the drill bit at the required length so you know when to stop (see below). To prevent slippage when drilling laminate, start the hole with a bradawl or nail.

Drilling a large hole in a dowel

Screw a length of 1 x 2in. (25 x 50mm.) batten, wide side down, to a wider length of scrap wood as above. Position the dowel below the batten and secure, using a large C-clamp. This simple device will hold a dowel firmly without slippage while you work. The illustration to the right shows a flat wood (or spade) bit in use.

USING POWER TOOLS

- Use circuit breaker to cut off current in case saw or drill should cut cable.
- Ban children and pets from working area.
- Check that blade is facing in right direction.
- Replace blunt blades and drill bits.
- Check that there is nothing underneath that could be cut by blade or bit.
- Wear goggles.
- Keep cable away from blade or bit.
- Switch off before removing from wood.
- Unplug tool when not in use or when changing blades and bits.

PLANNING

Most of the planning tools and materials we use are very basic. In many cases the traditional carpenters' and graphite pencils shown below could be replaced with a thick, soft lead pencil. Layout and tracing paper are available in various sizes and can be found in art supply stores. So can the wonderful appliqué film (see opposite). Graph paper is a help when checking design proportions or planning adapations of your own. Use a scale of 1:12 if working with standard measurements; 1:10 is more convenient if working with the metric system. For space reasons we don't show our larger straightedge—a 6ft. 6in. (2m.)-long piece of 2 x 1in. (50 x 25mm.) pine kept strictly for drawing long, straight lines. There are various ways to check the right angles on guide lines for painted panels, moldings, and grid patterns—including T-squares and try squares—but we think a right-angled triangle is one of the cheapest solutions and all you need for our projects. A spirit level is vital, too, if marking the position, for example, of wall fittings; there's one illustrated on page 27.

PLANNING TOOLS A metal ruler, a good straightedge (but beware—it can be bent or twisted); an extending metal ruler; graph, tracing, and layout papers; colored pencils, useful for hiding the grid lines for roller patterns; marker pen; carpenters', and (far right) graphite pencils, both for marking wood; china marker for marking dark surfaces, glass, and fabric; a right-angled triangle.

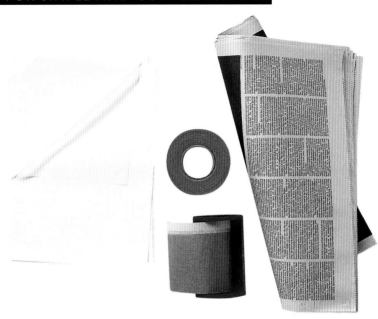

USING MASKS FOR SIMPLE AND COMPLEX SHAPES

MATERIALS
Newspaper, the cheapest way to protect the area around a stencil when using sprays; low-tack brown paper painter's tape, a good way to create straight-sided shapes; masking tape, available in various widths (but remove some of the tack if using on paint); appliqué film, the most expensive and most flexible mask (see below)

Using painter's tape

1 Two strips were cut and stuck down horizontally, with the adhesive edges (see right) to the edges of the rectangle. Two other strips were positioned vertically in the same way.

2 To remove, hold the paper sections and pull gently so the tape does not disturb the sprayed paint. When working with multiple strips, make sure to remove them in reverse order. This secure system is cheaper than masking tape.

Using appliqué film

This matte, low-tack film with a translucent paper backing enables you to create curved or intricate masks by tracing directly onto the film. It is available in several sizes. Simply place it over your chosen design, trace the outline, cut out with an X-Acto knife, carefully peel off the backing, and position. The pineapple was composed of several pieces, but I retained the background, too, so I had two options—to mask all but the fruit or just the fruit. You can also draw shapes straight onto the film.

MIXING COLOR

Most of the paint, glaze, and wash colors featured on our painted projects are mixed from a base of latex flat paint, tinted with water-based artists' acrylic colors (available in tubes in a wide range of shades under standard names). I like to work with latex flat because it is easy and safe to use, quick to dry, and almost odor-free.

Although I choose to mix most of my colors when working with latex flat, there are occasions when I opt for premixed tones. The exceptions are the deep reds, oranges, yellows, and blues, and the coats used before and after crackle varnish. Deep tones require so much color if mixed from a white base that the paint's plasticity is compromised—that is, it no longer flows properly. Similarly, water-based crackle varnish can't work its intended magic (see page 148) when the paint above and below it is behaving unpredictably. The alternative when you plan to use strong tones could be to go for a base nearer to the color you want. But strong colors are the most fugitive, so I often prefer to avoid the risk of upsetting the composition of the paint.

It's easy to modify the colors I suggest and to experiment with your own. Add each ingredient in stages, stir well, and check the effect as you go. Black and white will darken or lighten some colors but shades of gray create subtler results, and you can add a little water (or thinner) to help the paint flow more easily. Keep records of what you do and mix slightly more than you think you need. Manufacturers estimate that 1 quart (1 liter) of latex flat covers 11–18yd.^{2} (9–15m.^{2}). Actual coverage varies according to usage and surface. Added color and glazing liquid make no real difference.

Most period color ranges are available in latex paint. Seek advice from the manufacturer on coloring agents for unusual paints. If you want to use an eggshell base, the coloring agent, too, must be oil-based; use mineral spirit to thin. Don't try color mixing with gloss paints.

MIXING FROM A WHITE BASE Shades of artists' acrylic color were added to white latex flat paint to create both colors: (left) monestial and emerald greens; cadmium and lemon yellows.

MIXING FROM A DARK BASE
Start from a dark base if you want a dark color. Here the cadmium red of the center finial has been modified (left) to a warm, mid-range brown with Payne's gray, while (right) burnt umber has created a darker, earthier tone. Much smaller quantities of grays and umbers are also used to reduce color intensity.

WASHES, WAXES, AND GLAZES
A pale blue artists' color was mixed with (left to right) water, furniture wax, and transparent acrylic glazing liquid for three very different effects (and tones). Acrylic color was used for finials 1 and 3, but working with wax entailed a switch to oil. Note the grain visible through the wash on finial 1. Glazing liquid also makes paint appear translucent, an effect utilized in the colorwash finish on finial 3.

MEDIUM	COLOR WITH	THIN WITH
WATER-BASED		
• Latex flat paint • Latex semigloss paint • Acrylic glazing liquid • Acrylic varnishing wax	• Artists' acrylic color	• Water
OIL-BASED		
• Furniture wax	• Artists' oil color	• Mineral spirit

SPECIALIST PAINTS

Gilding doesn't have to mean "gold." You can achieve convincing silver, copper, and bronze finishes with the leaf, paint, cream, and bronze powders I use in our projects. Materials have improved enormously in the past few years. If you decide to use imitation metal leaf, be sure to buy the loose type. The kind that is mounted on film is difficult to handle. I'm rapidly becoming a spray-paint freak, too. Applied lightly and evenly and sealed with an appropriate varnish, spray paints are the best way to cover difficult surfaces like plastic laminate. If you have difficulty finding products locally, consult the suppliers list on page 188—many companies have mail-order services.

FABRIC COLORS
Fabric paints come in liquid or pen forms. Liquid forms are available in a range of colors and effects (opaque, translucent, or textured) and can be applied with a fine artists' or stencil brush. Pen forms are just like markers. Both must be sealed with an iron on the reverse. Dyes are made for cold-water hand or machine washing (see page 94).

WORKING WITH SPRAY PAINTS

Diffused color

A soft-edged look can be achieved with two steady, sweeping strokes, but don't press hard. Hold the can 12in. (30 cm.) from the surface.

Solid color

You need up to ten sweeping strokes for such opaque coverage. Again, don't be tempted to press hard. Aim for a series of light, even coats.

WORKING WITH GILDED FINISHES

MATERIALS
From the left: Loose imitation gold (Dutch metal) leaf, made from three cheaper metals and

available in various tones, here interleaved for easier use; gold leaf paint, expensive because it is

powdered gold in a medium but economical to use; bronze powders for gold, copper, and bronze effects (in

paper packs and tube)—masks are essential when using them; gilt cream, a good alternative to leaf,

easy to apply, and available in various tones; silver and gold acrylic paint, easy to use and quick drying

Applying imitation metal leaf

1 Using a fitch, brush an even coat of size onto the areas you intend to gild. Wait until the size becomes clear and tacky (15–20 minutes).

2 Lift each leaf carefully, making sure you pick up only one at a time, and place on the sized area. Smooth and then burnish, working gently with a soft-bristled brush or dust cloth.

PAINTING EQUIPMENT

Most of the tools I use in our projects are inexpensive and can be bought from a hardware store or home center if you don't already have them. Some of the pure bristle brushes are more costly; for these you'll need to go to a specialist supplier. It's worth assembling a basic kit so that you can tackle most makeovers easily. Use the equipment specified for a technique or you may not achieve the intended effect. Ordinary synthetic sponges, for example, have their uses, but when a project asks for natural sponges it is worth spending a little more. You can, however, make savings on the number of brushes I specify by cleaning the brush used for a previous stage and doubling up.

With care, good brushes will last a long time. Clean them thoroughly. For water-based materials, rinse under running water, wash in soapy water, and rinse again. Then rub the bristles between your palms inside a soft plastic bag, reshape while damp, and hang to dry. For oil-based materials, dip and rinse in denatured alcohol, squeezing hard to clean, then washing in soapy water, rinsing, and reshaping as above. Some specialist paints require paint thinners for cleaning—I also recommend thinners to clean tin when finishing. Use with great care, and follow the manufacturer's instructions for storage.

CLOTHS, SPONGES, AND ROLLERS Stockinette, sold on the roll—ideal for applying waxes; a lint-free cotton cloth, also used for applying waxes and for removing excess paint and glaze; natural sponges, whose irregular texture creates attractive effects when used to apply paint or glaze to wood or fabric; a synthetic sponge and two sponge replacements for paint rollers, useful for improvised stamps; a wallpaper seam roller, the easiest way to create stripes

BRUSHES FOR SURFACES

From the top: two round hoghair brushes, good for stippling and for textural finishes; a varnish brush, expensive and best kept for acrylic varnishes; two latex brushes, whose especially flexible bristles are ideal for applying water-based paint; two tossaway brushes—basic, stiff-bristled brushes for gloss paint, oil-based varnish, and "dirty jobs"; metal and plastic paint kettles, indispensable containers—use the plastic, lidded type for storing water-based paints and glazes; mixing sticks, a good use for scrap wood

BRUSHES FOR DECORATION

From top left: three stencil brushes—inexpensive, so it's good to keep a range of sizes; selection of five small artists' brushes, plus (the longest) a round fitch—all are good for freehand painting, and the fitch is also used to apply wax resist and glue; a lining brush, whose long, pure bristles are best when painting long, straight, thin lines; two soft-bristled brushes, used to apply imitation metal leaf and bronze powders

STAMPS, STENCILS, AND DECOUPAGE

There are no surprises in the materials and equipment lists for these familiar techniques, and everything you need can be found in any crafts or art supply store.

Rubber stamps are now available in a huge range of designs and styles and offer an attractive, easy option if you want to decorate painted (or unpainted) surfaces. You can apply liquid stamp paints with a roller, but I much prefer the water-based ink stamp pads for fabric which work on wood, metal, and plastics as well and make the best impressions. See page 164 for more about stamps, bought and improvised.

An X-Acto knife (or craft knife) and cutting mat are essential when making stencils. You can cut them from paper, thin cardboard, or oiled-manilla stencil paper. Stencil paper, available in various sizes, is obviously the most expensive, but it is the strongest and certainly worth buying if you plan to use a design frequently. If you have linseed oil on hand, you could try sealing plain light cardboard for yourself, but make sure it is completely dry before you use it.

Découpage depends for its impact largely on the materials you choose. Dover Publications produce invaluable compilations of out-of-copyright material, and, as the screen on page 8 suggests, there's a wealth of contemporary ephemera just begging to be exploited.

STAMPS
Rubber stamps will produce hard-wearing results on any prepared and painted surface if you use a water-based fabric ink stamp pad and seal. Subtle colors are available, and the stamps are easily cleaned with soapy water. Use the plain end of a sponge roller for a perfect dot.

USING REGISTER MARKS FOR STENCILS

Note the aligning pencil marks at the top. The lower one indicates the center top of the basic white vase shape and was transferred from the stencil to the shape once the paint had dried. Its position is important because you must be able to align the first mark with the one on the second stencil once that is in position. Registration marks have also been added at the sides and center bottom. All will be concealed by the second stencil color.

AGING EFFECTS FOR DÉCOUPAGE

Discoloration
Prepare tea, using two bags to each half cup of water. Cool without stirring. Pour off the liquid and wipe the whole surface or just the découpage with the bags.

Age spots
Make instant coffee, using 2tbsp. to a half cup of water. Again, cool without stirring. Pour most of the liquid away and flick some of the granules over the surface.

MOSAIC AND TIN

Mosaic tiles are commonly available in two forms—either in single color batches mounted on a paper backing or in bags of assorted colors. You could substitute ceramic wall or floor tiles, or even pottery, but think twice before mixing them with mosaic tiles if you want a level surface, as for a table. It is possible to combine varying thicknesses, but it's a time-consuming business. Make sure to use ceramic tile adhesive so that you can vary the depth of the bed in which you lay them, and check constantly with a spirit level.

Pure tin is not readily available, nor is it necessary for our technique. For the French Dresser on page 70 we used tin-plated steel, a tougher material which you are unlikely to pierce. Some craft stores carry it, but builders' suppliers may be the best local source. The alternative is a specialist metal supplier; check the phone book for the nearest. Zinc is a substitute (see page 178) and is more generally available from builders' suppliers. Tin and zinc are milled in various thicknesses (or gauges), so make sure your supplier understands how you intend to use them.

PUNCHING DESIGNS ON TIN

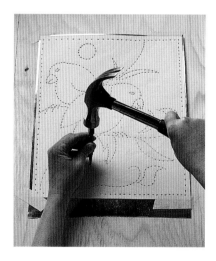

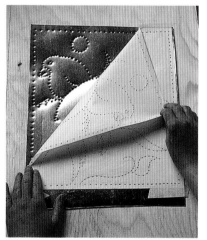

1 Use masking tape to secure the tin to a piece of particleboard and the traced design to the tin. Place the center punch on one of the lines, hold upright, and tap gently with the hammer.

2 Reposition the center punch and continue working in the same way. Your aim is to dent the surface, not pierce it. The claw hammer could be replaced with a lighter tack hammer.

VARIATIONS
In these very typical motifs, large and small center punches have been supplemented with the tip of a single-slot screwdriver. You can try varying the spaces between the holes, too.

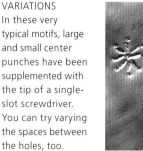

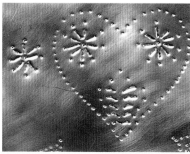

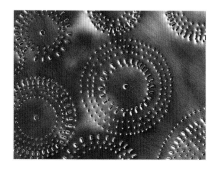

WORKING WITH MOSAIC TILES

MATERIALS
Sheets of mosaic tiles (or tesserae), mounted on brown paper; small, hand-fired ceramic wall tiles, a possible alternative; tile nippers with a spring-handled operation, much the easiest to use; a selection of colors; ready-mixed grout (left) and ceramic tile adhesive—simpler to use than powdered varieties. Alternative adhesive (not shown): clear, strong PVA (polyvinyl acetate) glue.

1 Once you have drawn the basic outline on the chosen surface, begin gluing the whole background tiles in place. Work from the corners and the outside edges inward. For this project a clear, strong PVA glue was used to attach and protect the tiles.

2 Using the nippers, trim tiles to complete the background and glue in place. Then lay pieces to form the motif. I cut mine by hand, but you can smash them (see page 176).

VARNISHES AND WAXES

The sealant or protective coat can affect the look of your makeover so profoundly that it's vital you choose the right product. When adapting our makeovers or designing your own, there are several basic questions to ask yourself. Will the piece be used indoors or out? If outdoors, avoid waxes and go for marine varnish. If indoors, how much protection do you want? Finishes in kitchens and bathrooms need a lot; as do those in children's rooms, where it's safest to opt for water-based products. Lastly, what is the final effect to be? Use matte varnish or wax (but don't buff) for a surface that feels natural. For a natural look, choose the low-sheen varnishes or waxes, bearing in mind that beeswax yellows and that tinted waxes (see Decoration) alter the underlying color as well as sealing, sometimes for an aging effect, so run trials first. Remember: there are times and places in which it may be right to do without, as for the Bleached Wardrobe on page 51, where I wanted a "raw" look.

PROTECTION

VARNISH TYPE	MEDIUM	HEAT RESISTANT	WATER RESISTANT	DURABILITY	SHEEN/ GLOSS	NON YELLOWING	PROJECT USED
Acrylic varnish *applied with brush* clear flat	Ⓦ	✓	✓	▲	Low	✓	Metal Trunks—Verdigris and Gingham
clear matte	Ⓦ	✓	✓	▲	None	✓	Wardrobe Shelving Fabric Headboards— Moorish
clear satin	Ⓦ	✓	✓	▲	Mid	✓	Wardrobe Doors—Gilded Drawers—Stenciled and Renaissance Gilded Table
Acrylic varnish *spray form* clear satin	Ⓦ	✓	✓	◆	Mid	✓	Laminated Kitchen Units Dining Chairs—Metallic Loom Chairs
Lacquer varnish *spray form* clear gloss	⊙	✓	✓	◆	High	✓	Fridge-Freezer (see p.91)
Polyurethane varnish *applied with brush* clear matte	⊙	✓	✓	◆	None	✗	Café Tables (alternative for indoor use—see below)
Marine varnish *applied with brush* clear matte	⊙	✓	✓	◆	None	✗	Café Tables (exterior use)

PROTECTION

WAX TYPE	MEDIUM	HEAT RESISTANT	WATER RESISTANT	DURABILITY	SHEEN/ GLOSS	NON YELLOWING	PROJECT USED
Acrylic varnishing wax *applied with brush or cloth* clear	Ⓦ	✓	✓	◆	Mid	✓	Dining Chairs—Rush Seat and Fifties Retro Giverny Chair
Beeswax polish *applied with cloth*	Ⓞ	✓	✓	▲	Mid	✗	French Dresser
Furniture wax or polish *applied with cloth* clear	Ⓞ	✓	✓	▲	Mid	✓	Wardrobe Doors—Country French Dresser Console Tables Fabric Headboards—Shaker
Transparent wax *applied with cloth* clear	Ⓞ	✓	✓	▲	Mid	✓	Flexible Storage (casters) Four-poster

DECORATION

VARNISH TYPE	MEDIUM	HEAT RESISTANT	WATER RESISTANT	DURABILITY	METHOD
Crackle varnish *applied with brush*	Ⓦ	✓	✓	▲	Apply between base and top coats to create a crazed, aged-paint effect.
Etch cream *applied with brush and roller*	Ⓦ	✓	✓	◆	Apply to clear glass to reproduce the appearance of etching. Tint with colorizers.

WAX TYPE

WAX TYPE	MEDIUM	HEAT RESISTANT	WATER RESISTANT	DURABILITY	METHOD
Acrylic varnishing wax *applied with brush or cloth*	Ⓦ	✓	✓	◆	Tint with artists' acrylic color to create an even, colored stain/sealant. Buff for mid sheen.
Furniture wax or polish *applied with cloth*	Ⓞ	✓	✓	▲	Tint with artists' oil color to create an aging, colored polish/sealant. Buff for mid sheen. Also used for aged-paint resist technique (applied with small fitch).
Liming wax *applied with cloth*	Ⓞ	✓	✓	▲	Apply to unpainted or painted wood to create soft, bleached effect as paste is retained in the grain when excess wiped off. Buff for mid sheen.

Ⓦ = water-based
Ⓞ = oil-based
▲ = suitable for average wear and tear (use in living room or bedroom)
◆ = suitable for heavy wear and tear (use in bathroom or kitchen)

FITTINGS

Never pass up a chance to sift through the handles, knobs, and finials in any store. You don't have to spend a lot to find quirky fittings that can be the starting point for a makeover. The secret is not to think of them simply as finishing touches, and remember you can always paint, spray, or decorate the fitting itself. I've tapped painted upholstery nails into painted wooden handles in a simple daisy motif to lift a simple set of drawers. If you want a traditional look, most home centers hold a basic range of shapes, and there are specialist companies that offer more extensive selections.

Experiment with found objects, too. Shells and driftwood, for example, can be used to great effect. Find the right shape, and either could feature as designer pulls in a makeover for a bathroom cabinet. I'd use epoxy glue to mount the shell on a concealed dowel and screw that into position. I've also turned old soupspoons into fun handles on a kitchen cabinet. Bend into a comfortable shape using pliers, drill a hole at either end, and secure, using countersunk screws.

PREVIEW
Some of the most striking handles from our projects: 1 designer chrome, certainly the most expensive; 2 and 3 chain-store plastic, sprayed silver; 4 more of the same, this time with a copper spray; 5 chrome handles teamed with traditional brass card holders—a surprising combo which works partly because of the bright yellow I used for the high-gloss lacquer finish.

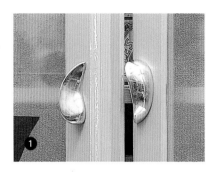

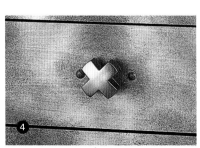

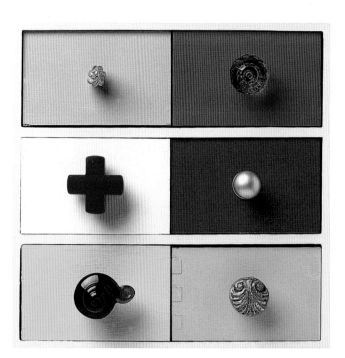

RAW MATERIALS
This unpainted set of drawers seemed the perfect way to demonstrate a few of the budget-range handles now on the market. Each one suggests various treatments. What about that red cross on the little mobile bedside table below?

FANCY FINIALS
We use them on a four-poster, for tiebacks, and for fabric headboards. Wood, glass, and metal—they are full of possibilities.

SIMPLE ADD-ONS
Add period legs or casters to this little bedside unit and it changes character instantly. The aged-paint finish survives its original makeover (see page 64), but the wild contrast here leaves me wanting to explore two very different looks.

PART TWO

FACELIFTS

Detailed step-by-step instructions for an inspiring and wide-ranging collection of makeovers for every room in your home, as well as ten pages of themed ideas for you to explore and develop for yourself

Bright, modern colors allied to some vigorous aging techniques make a dramatic statement with a simple, rough, old coffer. I like the mixture of textures created by the heavy crackle glaze applied to the top (see page 148) and the dusty, rubbed-back look of the wax-resist aged paint effect on the panels below (see page 144).

ABOUT FACELIFTS

Treat this section as a portfolio of suggestions reflecting the range of basic furniture types, from storage through tables and chairs to beds. Whether your style is country, fifties retro, chic minimalist, or downright romantic, there's a makeover solution here for you. Each of our major projects is presented with step-by-step instructions for construction or adaptation (where appropriate) and decoration, cross-referred to our detailed techniques section in Part Three. So, if you were lucky enough to find a very similar piece, you'd have a complete guide to making our transformation for yourself, plus, in most instances, at least one alternative colorway. But that's not how we hope

you'll use this book. It's really a collection of mix and match options to coordinate in creating pieces that work for the way you live your life.

To take an example, let's imagine that your dream home boasts a perfectly adequate kitchen by an unimaginative designer.

For straightforward paint solutions, have a look at page 88 for our update on laminated units, or the copper effect on page 93—another modern approach, but one that could accent a single cabinet in a series of colorwashed units, too. For a stunning treatment that teams an aged paint technique with the simple crafts of punched tin and frosted glass, look at the

Left: This rustic cupboard with a Mediterranean feel is a clever assembly job prompted by the acquistion of some lovely old shutters. But look at the base— the drawer is set in a pretty flared and scalloped shape which could be jigsawed out to conceal much plainer legs. Woodwashes in tones of blue and green (see page 140) give it a sunbleached look.

Opposite: There are several very interesting ideas to borrow here. Note the simple, effective use of Chinese characters (these could be hand painted or decoupaged— see page 160), the striking "handles" (semicircular sections cut and mounted on the door fronts), the tiny corner detail on the door panels, and the steel pulls chosen to reflect the style of the piece.

French café look we've contrived for a junk-shop dresser with paneled doors (see page 70). We added a zinc top too—easy to fit following our instructions—but maybe not right for you.

If you're willing to try a very simple adaptation, take another look at those kitchen doors. If they are flat, why not add a handsome molding, and maybe change the handles on some doors and remove others completely, adding pretty fabric to the shelves and shades or curtains at the open fronts? You could easily adapt our wardrobe shelving project on page 60, using a printed vinyl fabric on the shelves; and the gilded wardrobe project on page 52 can tell you all about using moldings.

If you're game for a little more simple do-it-yourself, there's the country-style wardrobe on page 54—a very different approach to storage cupboards and another for flat doors. You could opt for single "windows" and a natural look with the pale colorway illustrated on page 151, plus inserts of cream on white gingham.

I've started and it's hard to stop, but I'm sure you'll have taken the point. Make time to look through all the projects—even those that don't seem relevant—so you know what can be achieved given some very rewarding time and effort.

Don't be put off by those that contain an element of construction. I am lucky enough to have a partner who translates my ideas into practice, but I am confident that we have come up with pieces that combine good looks with achievable results. The methods are basic, the tools

easy to use, and the skill level minimal. When we began, my confidence was low; but I promise you that if I can do what's required— and I can—then anyone can. Those first nervous cuts with the jig saw are long behind me now. If you, too, are inexperienced, it makes sense to study the advice in Part One and work on your basic skills first. If the idea still fills you with dread, your lumberyard may be the answer.

Most will cut wood to size and jigsaw shapes to a template. Just be clear what you want before you go.

Lastly, some practical advice. Read all the instructions, including cross-references, before you shop. Be aware that your measurements will almost inevitably differ from ours, and that this will affect the dimensions of materials like wood, metal, and fabric plus paint quantities. Adjust your shopping list accordingly.

Kitsch glamour in a fun, fashionable interior which owes a lot to Hollywood in the thirties. Wooden inserts, strip molding, and corrugated iron transform some nondescript seating, while a mixture of metal leaf gilding and metallic paint (see page 168) puts on the razzle dazzle. It's not furniture, I know, but I think the galvenized metal makeover on the old fireplace is a stunningly simple solution to a knotty problem.

WARDROBE DOORS

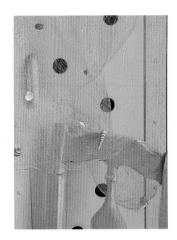

These three projects illustrate how simple it is to give completely different identities to the same basic piece of furniture. In this case, I've used a plain free-standing wardrobe made of particleboard with a white plastic finish— a practical object for any room in which existing closets are no longer sufficient to hold all the things you need to store. The first wardrobe, for example, could go into a large bathroom and hold towels and bathroom clutter; the second could embellish an elegant bedroom; the third would enhance a country-style kitchen. You could adapt these same ideas to any bland-looking cabinets you already possess to integrate them into your decor.

BLEACHED AND BATTERED

CLEANING AND PRIMING

Clean the surface thoroughly before and after construction; prime the doors (inside and out) and the exterior shell. See pages 12–17.

MATERIALS

Preparation ▶ ¼in. (6mm.) plywood or MDF, precut to size (see below)
Construction ▶ 7 fl. oz. (210ml.) wood glue / 12 finishing nails / approx. 150 dome-headed upholstery nails / 1 fl. oz. (30ml.) quick-dry epoxy glue
Base coat ▶ 1 pint (500ml.) white latex flat paint
Wax resist ▶ 5 fl. oz. (150ml.) furniture wax (clear)
Top coats ▶ 13 fl. oz. (380ml.) white latex flat paint / 10 fl.oz. (300ml.) turquoise artists' acrylic color / 3½ fl. oz. (100ml.) monestial green artists' acrylic color (2 coats)

EQUIPMENT

Fittings ▶ 2 round mirrors (wood frame) / 2 nautical knobs and screws
screwdriver / metal rule / right-angled triangle / ruler or straightedge / pencil / adjustable workbench and/or C-clamps / protective mask (if using MDF) / jigsaw / medium- and fine-grade sandpaper / 2 x 1in. (25mm.) round fitches / tack hammer / masking tape / scissors / drill with flat wood bit / mixing sticks / 2 x 2in. (50mm.) latex brushes / container to mix glaze / lint-free cotton rags / water to dampen rags

INSTRUCTIONS

Preparation

ALWAYS WEAR A MASK IF CUTTING MDF.

1 Remove the doors and knobs carefully, using the appropriate screwdriver. Reserve the hinges and their screws.
2 The simplest way to make the door frames is to cut each of them in one piece from wooden board and mount them on the existing doors. Use the metal rule, triangle, ruler (or straightedge), and pencil to draw the outlines on both pieces of precut wood—the width of your frames will depend on your door and mirror sizes. With 14in. (36cm.) doors and 9½in. (24.5cm.) mirrors, we opted for frames 2in. (5cm.) wide.

3 Secure one piece of wood with clamps, cut out the central section, using the jig-saw; discard. Repeat for other frame. Sand edges, with medium-grade sandpaper.

Construction

1 Using one of the fitches, apply a thin layer of wood glue to one side of each frame and position on the outside of the doors.

2 Tap finishing nails into each frame, one at each corner and one halfway down the long sides. Decorate with rows of upholstery nails.

3 Sand the mirror frames, back and front, with medium-grade sandpaper.

4 Decide on the height of the mirrors, and glue in place with epoxy glue.

5 Mask the glass with tape to protect from paint splashes. Tap upholstery nails around frames.

6 Using the flat wood bit, drill random holes below the mirrors.

Aged paint finish

See page 144, Wax Resist. The battered, bleached look of the aqua-on-white doors entailed lots of sanding with fine-grade sandpaper, and I omitted a sealant coat to enhance the effect.

Final assembly

Screw on the new handles and rehang the doors.

GILDED GLAMOUR

CLEANING AND PRIMING

Prepare the surface by cleaning before and after construction; prime the doors (inside and out) and the exterior shell. See pages 12–17.

MATERIALS

Preparation ▸ deep frame molding, mitered to size (see opposite)
Construction ▸ 7 fl. oz. (210ml.) wood glue / finishing nails
Base/top coats ▸ 13 fl. oz. (380ml.) white latex flat paint / 10 fl. oz. (300ml.) turquoise artists' acrylic color / 3½ fl. oz. (100ml.) monestial green artists' acrylic color
Size coat ▸ 10 fl. oz. (300ml.) water-based size
Gilding ▸ 30–40 loose sheets aluminum leaf
Sealant coat ▸ 1 pint (500ml.) satin acrylic varnish (clear)
Aging glaze ▸ 5 fl. oz. (150ml.) acrylic glazing liquid (transparent) / 5 fl. oz. (150ml.) white latex flat paint / 3½ fl. oz. (100ml.) turquoise artists' acrylic color / 5tsp. monestial green artists' acrylic color
Fixings ▸ 2 scroll handles with screws

EQUIPMENT

Screwdriver / graph paper / pencil / metal rule / ruler or straightedge / right-angled triangle / 1 x ½in. (12mm.) round fitch / tack hammer / 2 containers for mixing paint and glaze / mixing sticks / 2 x 2 in. (50mm.) latex brushes / masking tape / scissors / lint-free cotton rags / 1 x 1 in. (25mm.) flat bristle brush / disposable gloves / soft-bristled brush or clean dustcloth / 1 x 2 in. (50mm.) varnish brush

INSTRUCTIONS
Preparation

1 See Bleached Doors, Preparation, step 1, on page 50.

2 Mitering equipment is expensive to buy—although it can be rented—and difficult to use if you are inexperienced. By far the simplest solution is to get your chosen molding mitered by your supplier. Picture-framers will sometimes do the work for you, but you will probably have to buy the wood elsewhere. (Obviously, you need four short pieces and four long ones.) Whoever cuts the wood will need the final dimensions of the panels you want to create, so measure your doors and decide where you want to place your molding before you have it mitered. Draw a scale plan on graph paper to check fit. For maximum impact I chose a molding with a very deep profile and set it 1 in. (2.5 cm.) from the edge of the door.

Construction

1 Mark the appropriate guide lines on each panel, using a pencil, ruler (or straightedge), and right-angled triangle.

2 Brush a thin, even coat of glue onto the back of one of the short pieces, using the fitch, and position at the top of one door. Working clockwise, glue the remaining three pieces. Repeat for the other door.

3 Secure each length with evenly spaced finishing nails tapped gently into the molding with the hammer.

Base and top coats

1 Pour the white latex paint into one of the containers, add the turquoise and monestial green, and stir well.

2 Apply two even coats to the prepared and primed surfaces with a latex brush, allowing 2–3 hours for each coat to dry.

Gilding the molding

See page 168 for the technique, but omit the base and sealant coats. I masked the surrounding areas with tape, then I applied the size, taking some of the tack off on a clean rag first, and aimed for complete coverage when gilding, using fragments to patch.

Sealant coat

Stir the varnish well and apply to the doors, inside and out, and to the shell, using the varnish brush. Allow to dry (2–3 hours).

Aging the molding

See page 147, Aging with Glaze, for the technique. Remask the surrounding areas before you begin, and quickly rub off the excess glaze with clean rags folded to form a pad. Allow to dry (1 hour) and remove the masking tape.

Final assembly

See Bleached Doors.

COUNTRY CHIC

CLEANING AND PRIMING

Prepare the surface by cleaning before and after construction; prime the doors (inside and out) and the exterior shell. See pages 12–17.

MATERIALS

Base coats ▶ 25 fl. oz. (740ml.) premixed deep red latex flat paint (2 coats)
Glaze coat ▶ 8½ fl. oz. (250ml.) acrylic glazing liquid (transparent) / 3⅓ tbsp. burnt umber artists' acrylic color
Sealant coat ▶ 7 fl. oz. (210ml.) furniture wax (clear)
Mesh ▶ chicken wire / 1¾ fl. oz. (50ml.) antique gold spray paint
Fitting the fabric ▶ approx. 2 yd. x 56 in. (2 m. x 140 cm.) tartan cotton 8 sash rods to fit openings / 16 hooks
Fittings ▶ 2 pre-patinated brass doorknobs

EQUIPMENT

Screwdriver / metal rule / ruler or straightedge / right-angled triangle / pencil / graph paper (optional) / adjustable workbench and/or C-clamps / jigsaw / mixing sticks / 2 x 2 in. (50 mm.) latex brushes / container for mixing glaze / lint-free cotton rags / tinsnips / newspaper to protect work surface / hand-held staple gun and appropriate staples / masking tape (optional) / bradawl / scissors / needle and thread

INSTRUCTIONS
Preparation

1 See Bleached Doors, Preparation, step 1.
2 Using the metal rule, ruler (or straightedge), triangle, and pencil, mark out the two openings for each door. Ours are the same size top and bottom—9 x 39in. (23 x 99cm.)— but taller ones at the bottom look good too. It's wise to draw designs to scale on graph paper before cutting.
3 Secure each door in turn with clamps, cut the upper and lower panels out carefully, using the jigsaw; discard.

Dragging

See page 150 for the technique. Here the two premixed red latex base coats were dragged with a darker red mix. When applying glaze to the doors, aim for long strokes, working vertically on the long sides and horizontally on the "cross members."

Sealant coat

Using clean rags folded into a pad, apply the furniture wax, leave to set (15 minutes), and buff up with another clean rag.

Fitting the mesh

1 Using the tinsnips, cut four sections of chicken wire to fit the openings in your doors, adding 1in. (2.5cm.) extra on all four sides.

2 Lay the pieces on the newspaper, and, using a sweeping movement, spray one side only with antique gold, holding the can approx. 12in. (30cm.) from the surface. Allow to dry (1 hour).

3 Position mesh on the reverse of the doors and staple in place at the top and bottom only, using horizontal rows of staples approx. ½in. (12mm.) from the edges. Secure the sides with masking tape while you work if you prefer.

Fitting the fabric

1 Making the initial hole with the bradawl, screw a hook beside each corner of the mesh at every opening.

2 Cut out four pieces of fabric to match the openings, adding hem allowances of 2in. (5cm.) at the top and at the bottom of each piece and 4in. (10cm.) at each side. If you are afraid of fraying or insist on neat edges, hem the sides before beginning step 4.

3 Using the needle and thread, turn under and sew the top and bottom edges of each piece to create a casing or open-ended hem for the sash rod, making sure it will slip through the casing easily.

4 Thread the rods through the casings—the fabric gathers automatically—and hang the curtains from the hooks, adjusting the length of the rods to fit. To the "non-sewer" the last two steps may sound complicated. They really aren't—and this kind of fixing makes cleaning much simpler.

Final assembly

See Bleached Doors.

THREE WAYS WITH
A SET OF DRAWERS

Here's another makeover idea for budget-range furniture—in this case, a small chest made of particleboard. There's no adaptation involved—just a variety of painted surfaces and decorative effects and the replacement of some undistinguished wooden knobs. In fact, for the first and the third, it was the handles that dictated the treatment, and the result is two very different pieces. If I have a favorite, it's the one below, but I had been looking for a way to use these chrome handles for ages. The second is interesting, too. I was experimenting with ways of changing how we look at chests of drawers. A stencil inspired by a Ming vase turned almost Op Art in an attempt to assert a vertical view. It's an approach to adapt for a child's room, finding a fun way to use the knobs!

CONTEMPORARY GLOSS

CLEANING AND PRIMING

Remove the drawers and knobs, and prepare the shell and drawer fronts thoroughly by cleaning (see pages 12–17) and priming with an oil-based primer (see page 142).

MATERIALS

**Lacquer coats ▶ 1½ quarts (1.5 liters) premixed bright yellow high-gloss paint (5 coats)
Hardware ▶ 3 aluminum card holders with screws / 3 long chrome handles with washers and nuts**

EQUIPMENT

Mixing sticks / 2 x 2in. (50mm.) tossaway brushes / silicon carbide abrasive paper / lint-free cotton rags / warm soapy water / bradawl / drill with wood bits / screwdriver / pliers

INSTRUCTIONS
Lacquer effect

See page 142 for the technique. Do take the advice about appropriate surfaces seriously, and study your piece of furniture objectively before you commit to this technique. Battered pieces are just not worth the effort. If you have any doubts, choose another paint finish.

Fittings

1 Decide on the position of the card holders, use the bradawl and drill to make the required holes, and then screw the holders in place.
2 Position the new handles, drilling the necessary holes for each on the inside of the drawers, and secure by tightening each external washer and internal nut with the pliers.

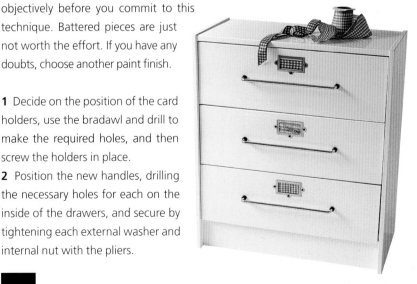

THREE WAYS WITH A SET OF DRAWERS

CLEANING AND PRIMING

Remove the drawers and knobs, and prepare the shell and drawer fronts thoroughly by cleaning and priming. See pages 12–17.

MATERIALS

Base and top coats ▶ 1 pint (500ml.) premixed bright yellow latex flat paint
Stencils ▶ 13 fl. oz. (380ml.) white latex flat paint / 4 fl. oz. (120ml.) cobalt blue artists' acrylic color
Sealant coats ▶ 1 pint (500ml.) clear satin acrylic varnish (2 coats)
Fittings ▶ 6 wooden knobs

EQUIPMENT

Mixing sticks / 1 x 2in. (50mm.) latex brush / photocopier / paper approx. 17 x 24in. (43 x 61cm.) stencil / masking tape / scissors / cutting mat / X-Acto knife / lint-free cotton rag / 2 saucers / 2 x 1in. (25mm.) stencil brushes / 2 small, round artists' brushes / container for mixing paint / 1 x 2in. (50mm.) varnish brush / screwdriver

INSTRUCTIONS
Base and top coats

Stir the latex paint well, and apply two even coats to the prepared and primed surfaces, allowing 2–3 hours for each coat to dry.

Stenciling

For the technique see page 159, Stippling; for the motifs, see page 182. First I stippled in the two vase shapes, then I painted the primed new knobs with one of the artists' brushes, using 8½ fl. oz. (250ml.) white latex paint. I mixed the deep blue second color in the container (using the remaining white latex paint and the cobalt blue), added the stripes with the second stencil, and painted parts of the knobs blue to complete the pattern. The stripe stencil was a useful guide here.

You need register marks to ensure that the two stencils align correctly. See the motifs on page 182 for instructions.

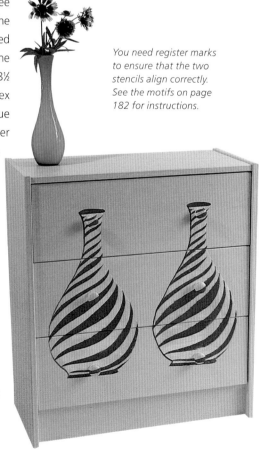

Sealant coats

Apply two coats of varnish, allowing 2–3 hours for each coat to dry.

Fittings

Screw the painted knobs in the original positions.

RENAISSANCE SPLENDOR

CLEANING AND PRIMING	Remove the drawers and knobs, and prepare the shell and drawer fronts thoroughly by cleaning and priming. See pages 12–17.
MATERIALS	Base coat ▶ 10 fl. oz. (300ml.) white latex flat paint / 1tbsp. dioxazine purple artists' acrylic color Glaze coats (dragging) ▶ 13 fl. oz. (380ml.) acrylic glazing liquid (transparent) / 1tbsp. dioxazine purple artists' acrylic color (3 coats) Découpage ▶ photocopies as required / 3½ fl. oz. (100ml.) purple water-based ink / 5tsp. water / 7 fl. oz. (210ml.) white glue Gilding ▶ 7 fl. oz. (210ml.) water-based size / approx. 3 loose sheets imitation gold (Dutch metal) leaf Sealant coats ▶ 1 pint (500ml.) clear satin acrylic varnish (2 coats) Fittings ▶ 6 large brass doorknobs
EQUIPMENT	Mixing sticks / 2 containers for mixing paint and glaze / 2 x 2in. (50mm.) latex brushes / water to dampen paper and cotton swabs / small, round artists' brush / 2 saucers / cotton swabs / natural sponge / newspaper / 1 x 1in. (25mm.) tossaway brush / cotton rag / disposable gloves / 1 x 1in. (25mm.) flat bristle brush / 1 x 1in. (25mm.) soft-bristled brush or clean dustcloth / 1 x 2in. (50mm.) varnish brush / screwdriver
INSTRUCTIONS **First and second dragging**	For the technique see page 150. I used two coats of dark purple glaze over the paler purple base coat, reserving the final third for later. Both colors were mixed in containers and stirred well.
Découpage	See page 161, Tinting with Water-based Inks, and basic recipe. The photocopies were tinted with a purple ink. (Ignore the base and sealant coats.)
Third dragging	Apply the third dragged coat, using reserved glaze.
Gilding	See page 168, Gilding with Metal Leaf, Size coat and Gilding only. I used small fragments of leaf, placing them randomly to give the effect of an extremely worn gilded surface.
Sealant coats and Fittings	See Stenciled Drawers. For a softer effect, use wax sealant.

WARDROBE SHELVING

This wardrobe was in a sad state when spotted in a junk shop. The shell was robust, but the door was broken beyond repair. The thirties detail was too good to miss, so I rescued it and decided to convert it into a shelf unit for the kitchen. Bright gingham-lined shelves, crackle glaze in a modern colorway, and some elegant fretwork trim have given it new flair. As a finishing touch, I added a roller shade in coordinating fabric. You can have one made to your specifications by a decorator, or use a readymade shade. These are available in various widths at hardware store and home centers. The store will cut a shade to fit, if necessary. But you could equally well just leave the shelves open to display your dishes.

CLEANING AND PRIMING

Prepare the surface thoroughly by cleaning before and after construction; prime inside, outside, and shelves. See pages 12–17.

MATERIALS

Preparation ▶ 3½ fl. oz. (100ml.) fine ready-mixed wood filler / ¼in. (6mm.) plywood or MDF for new shelf, precut to required size (see below) / ½ x ¾in. (12 x 19mm.) battens for side and back / ¾ x 3½in. (19 x 87mm.) batten for front edge / readymade decorative fretwork
Construction ▶ 5 fl. oz. (150ml.) wood glue / 15 screws / 1¾ fl. oz. (50ml.) fine ready-mixed wood filler
Base coat ▶ 25 fl. oz. (740ml.) premixed bright blue latex flat paint
Crackle coat ▶ 20 fl. oz. (600ml.) acrylic crackle varnish (transparent)
Top coat ▶ 25 fl. oz. (740ml.) premixed bright green latex flat paint
Sealant coats ▶ 1 quart (1 liter) clear matte acrylic varnish (2 coats)
Covering the shelves ▶ 4⅜yd. x 56in. (4m. x 140cm.) cotton gingham / 10 fl. oz. (300ml.) fabric glue
Fixing the shade (optional) ▶ readymade roller shade, cut to size / 2 fl. oz. (60 ml.) wood glue / 4 finishing nails

EQUIPMENT

Screwdriver / filling knife / medium-grade sandpaper / metal rule / adjustable workbench and/or C-clamps / backsaw / drill with wood bits / 1 x ½in. (15mm.) round fitch / ruler or straightedge / spirit level / pencil / mixing sticks / 2 x 3in. (75mm.) latex brushes / 1 x 2in. (50mm.) brush / 1 x 2in. (50mm.) varnish brush / iron / scissors / large plate / thick cardboard to spread glue / lint-free cotton rags / container for mixing glaze / natural sponge / water to dampen and rinse sponge / 3 saucers / 2 x 1⅜in. (35mm.) diameter sponges for mini-roller / 2 small artists' brushes / bradawl / pliers

INSTRUCTIONS
Preparation

1 Remove the door hinges and the door.
2 Fill the hinge holes with ready-mixed wood filler (applied with the filling knife), allow to dry (1 hour), and sand.
3 Carefully unscrew the three supporting back and side battens for the original shelf, and remove it. The pieces are to be used as a pattern for the second shelf.

4 Ask your lumberyard to cut a piece of wood to size for the new shelf.

5 Measure the battens, and, securing the timber with clamps, cut six new ones with the backsaw—it's wise to replace those on the original shelf, too.

6 In the same way and using the original shelf as a pattern, cut a batten for the underside of the front edge of the second shelf. A thick shelf looks so much more generous than a thin one.

7 Measure the width of the opening, and cut the piece of readymade fretwork to fit, allowing a 1in. (2.5cm.) overlap for fixing on either side. If you are including a shade, remember when choosing your design that it must be deep enough to conceal the shade mechanism. (You can cheat with extra beading, of course.)

Construction

1 Drill three equally spaced holes along the front edge of the second shelf.

2 Using the fitch, apply wood glue sparingly to one of the narrow sides of the front-edge batten. Position the batten carefully underneath the shelf, aligning it with the front edge. Clamp, secure with screws, and allow to dry (1 hour).

3 Decide on the position of the two shelves, remembering that the front-edge battens make the shelves look deeper than they are. With the help of the tape measure, ruler (or straightedge), and spirit level, draw clear pencil guidelines for the position of the supporting battens both inside and outside the unit.

4 Drill two screw holes for each of the supporting battens.

5 Starting with the back battens and working from the outside, glue each one in place and secure with two screws. Allow to dry (1 hour). It's best to enlist someone's help here.

6 Fill all the drill holes with wood filler and allow to dry (1 hour). Rub down with the sandpaper.

Crackle finish

See page 148 for this technique, which was applied only to the outside of the wardrobe and to one side of the fretwork. I used a premixed blue latex paint for the base coat, two coats of crackle varnish, and another premixed latex paint, in green, for the top coat. Although the green was brushed on vertically, the crackle effect was surprisingly variable. This is because the unit had been patch-mended in the past and the various woods reacted differently.

Sealant coats

Stir the varnish well, and apply one or two coats to the crackle finish, allowing 2–3 hours for each coat to dry.

Covering the shelves

1 Iron the gingham. Trust me—don't skip this step. It makes the job much easier.

2 Lay one of the shelves face down on the gingham, and use as a template to cut out a piece of fabric to cover, allowing 1in. (2.5cm.) for turning under at the back and sides. Before you cut the fabric for the front edge, fold it up and over the batten to decide on the correct allowance. Cut a second piece to match.

3 Measure the inside of the unit and cut out a series of manageable pieces to cover the sides, back, top, and bottom, again allowing 1in. (2.5cm.) along the edges. If it helps, draw a plan as a reminder of what fits where.

4 Pour a little of the fabric glue at a time onto the plate— it's much easier to control quantity in this way. Using a small piece of thick cardboard as a spreader, apply a thin, even coat to the tops of the shelves, their edges, and to the underside—just wide enough for the turned-under edges of the fabric.

5 Quickly put the fabric in place, overlapping, clipping carefully where required, and turning under for neatness. Because this fabric is thin and allows some glue to seep through, you should not need to add more. Smooth out any wrinkles with a clean rag before the glue dries.

6 To cover the inside of the unit, fit the top section(s) first, then the back, and finally those for the sides, repeating steps 4 and 5. Allow to dry (1 hour) before positioning the shelves.

Fixing the shade

1 Following the instructions with the shade, position the shade inside the opening so that it hangs in front of the shelves. If you wish, you could first trim the shade with a decorative tassel or with some braid to harmonize with the wardrobe.

2 Using wood glue and the fitch, glue the fretwork in place, and secure with four finishing nails.

ADAPTATION

Minimum tools/maximum imagination is the theme. Only the tall cabinet requires more than two tools—and, for the others, if your lumberyard will cut wood to fit, you can do without a saw, too. But it's the ways you adapt these very basic ideas to suit your needs that make them valuable. Take the plate rack, for example. Forget plywood and fretwork and aim for a classical effect, adding top and side panels or a cornice cut from molding. For the bathroom, try panels of driftwood. (See pages 42–3 for sealants.)

Left: We added legs and instant dignity to this squat bedside unit. It's amazing how often that simple trick works. Fake it with a few books to decide how tall the legs should be. We used four tops for newel posts, which we found at a large home center, and each came fitted with a double-ended screw to attach it to the base. Colorway: white acrylic primer; aged paint finish— blue on white (see page 144). I highlighted the detail on the legs with bands of turquoise latex flat paint.

Left: Here basic shelving turns country plate rack with the addition of ¼in (6mm) plywood panels and fretwork edging. All are secured with wood glue and finishing nails. The shells were attached before I primed (see page 116). Colorway: white acrylic primer; crackle finish (see page 148,) sides and front only —pink on yellow. I also dry brushed green latex paint on the yellow interior (to help it tone with the wall) and applied liming wax to the entire surface.

Left: A storage solution for the home worker who needs to integrate office and living space, this idea adapts the makeover on page 54. Two extra plywood shelves were added, supported on brackets, and the casters offer even more flexibility. But beware: it's vital to check your wardrobe base for stability before adding casters. Ours has a three-quarter section set back to create a plinth and requires a full-size base to make it safe to move around—casters must be placed at the corners. It is also sensible to store heaviest items at the bottom. And note: with see-through doors, the interior must be painted too. Colorway: white acrylic primer; exterior—water-based dragging (see page 150); interior—dragged glaze 8½oz (250ml) acrylic glazing liquid, 2tbsp Payne's gray, and 1½tbsp titanium white artists' acrylics); casters—metal primer, dragged as exterior.

Above: Don't ditch the drawers when you dump a chest too damaged to restore. We removed the knobs (just for painting) and added small plywood shelves and dividers, secured with wood glue and finishing nails. This, and the multi-coated finish, made a wall unit suitable for light storage in kitchen or bathroom. See pages 27–8 for fixings. Colorway: lacquer finish—medium blue and yellow high-gloss paints (see page 142).

FLEXIBLE STORAGE
FOR HOME WORKERS

A pair of stout modern casters, an easy paint technique, and some elementary joinery turned this unused pine blanket box into a hardworking piece of storage for a home worker desperate to keep documents and files separate from the everyday clutter of family life. It can be a chronic problem if you don't have the luxury of a room of your own, and few of us want to solve it by importing standard filing cabinets into our living spaces. One of the obvious joys of this solution is that its function is so easily concealed once work is over; the other is its mobility. I opted for two-color woodwashing to preserve the grain and match the simple construction of this pine box. If your box is already painted, you'll have to strip it first—or choose another finish.

CLEANING

Prepare the surface thoroughly by cleaning before and after construction. See pages 12–17. No priming is necessary.

MATERIALS

Preparation ▶ ¼in. (6mm.) steel rod twice front to back of chest / 1 x 1in. (25 x 25mm.) batten / ¾in. x 3ft. (20mm. x 1m.) rope
Construction ▶ 12 screws
First wash coat ▶ 7 fl. oz. (210ml.) white latex flat paint / 4tbsp. emerald green artists' acrylic color / 1tbsp. cadmium yellow artists' acrylic color / 1tbsp. pale olive green artists' acrylic color / 6 fl. oz. (180ml.) water
Second wash coat ▶ 9 fl. oz. (270ml.) white latex flat paint / 2tbsp. raw umber artists' acrylic color / 6 fl. oz. (180ml.) water
Base coat (bronzing) ▶ 4 casters with 4in. (10cm.)-diameter wheels, plate fixing with appropriate screws / 3½ fl. oz. (100ml.) green acrylic spray paint
Size coat ▶ 3½tbsp. water-based size
Bronzing ▶ 1tbsp. copper bronze powder
Protective coat (bronzing) ▶ 3½tbsp. transparent polish (clear)
Final assembly ▶ 4 large ornamental studs (optional) / ½tbsp. copper gilt cream

EQUIPMENT

Metal rule / adjustable workbench and/or C-clamps / small hacksaw / masking tape (optional) / pencil / backsaw / drill with wood and ¼in. (6mm.) and 1in. (25mm.) flat wood bits / medium-grade sandpaper / scissors / hanging file (to check fit) / screwdriver / 2 containers for washes / mixing sticks / 2 x 2in. (50mm.) latex brushes / lint-free cotton rags / large plate / disposable gloves / adjustable wrench / protective mask / drop cloth / 1 x 1in. (25mm.) flat bristle brush / small, flat artists' brush / small, soft-bristled brush / 1 x 1in. (25mm.) tossaway brush / dustcloth / tack hammer (for optional studs)

INSTRUCTIONS

Preparation

1 Measure the internal width of the chest, secure the steel rod with clamps, and cut two lengths to fit, using the small hacksaw. These will form the supports for your hanging files. Ours were 13in. (33cm.) long. You can mark the rod with masking tape as a guide. (The keen-eyed may notice an extra batten in the front corner. We added it to strengthen a damaged batten inside the box.)

2 Measure the internal depth, and, with the pencil, mark out four lengths on the batten. Clamp and cut, using the backsaw. Again, ours were 13in. (33cm.) long.

3 Clamping each batten in turn, mark and drill a hole through it, approx. 1in. (2.5cm.) from one end—we'll call this the top—using the ¼in. (6mm.) flat wood bit.

4 Again clamping each batten in turn, substitute a standard wood bit and drill three equally spaced screw holes.

5 Use the pencil to mark the position of the two rope holes at each end of the chest, and drill all four holes, using the 1in. (25mm.) flat wood bit. Our holes were approx. 4½in. (11.5cm.) apart and 4in. (10cm.) from the top of the chest. Smooth any rough edges with sandpaper.

6 Cut the rope in half, using the scissors.

Construction

1 To assemble the supports for your hanging files, push each rod into the top holes on a pair of battens.

2 Place both pairs inside the box, with the rods uppermost, positioning one pair at one end with a batten in each corner. Use a hanging file to determine the correct positions for the other pair, adjusting the battens until the hooks at each side of the file hang on the rods. Mark the position of all four battens. We wanted to use legal-size folders, so our rods were 15½in. (39cm.) apart.

3 Screw in the four battens, working from the inside.

Woodwashing

See page 140. I used two washes for the entire surface, inside and out (excluding the bottom), the first green and the second a creamy white. The rope pieces were woodwashed green, too. Wearing the disposable gloves, I poured a little of the wash onto the large plate and pressed a clean rag over it until it was saturated. Then, cupping the folded rag in one hand, I pulled the rope through it with a twisting action. Allow the standard drying time.

Bronzing the casters

PROTECT YOUR WORK SPACE WITH DROP CLOTHS BEFORE SPRAYING, WORK IN A WELL-VENTILATED AREA, AND WEAR A MASK.

See page 169, Using Bronze Powders, for the technique. I decided to spray the green base coat rather than paint—it was so much easier to get even coverage. Remove the wheels, using the wrench, first.

Final assembly

1 Reattach the wheels.

2 Turn the chest upside down and secure the casters at the four corners, using the hardware supplied and the wrench.

3 Knot one end of one piece of rope, and, working from the inside, thread the other end out through one hole and in through its adjacent hole. Allowing enough slack for a handle, knot the free end on the inside and trim off the excess. Repeat for the other handle.

4 If using decorative studs, hammer one at each corner of the outside lid.

5 To highlight detail and texture, apply a little copper gilt cream to the rope and studs with a clean rag. Leave to set (approx. 15 minutes) and buff up with another clean rag.

FRENCH DRESSER

I found the bottom of this secondhand dresser first; and the top, when it turned up, was a perfect fit. Both were soundly made from particleboard covered in a wood laminate. The surfaces were finished with an oak stain/varnish, also in excellent condition, so preparation was limited to a good sanding. Although associated with country kitchens, free-standing kitchen units can be easily adapted, as here, for a less rustic feel.

CLEANING AND PRIMING

Clean the surface thoroughly; prime most exterior surfaces (including battens), but not lower door panels. See pages 12–17.

MATERIALS

Preparation ▶ 1 fl. oz. (30ml.) silver metallic car spray paint
Base coat ▶ 11 fl. oz. (320ml.) white latex flat paint / 3tbsp. raw umber artists' acrylic color
Wax resist ▶ 8½ fl. oz. (250ml.) furniture wax (clear)
Top coats ▶ 20 fl. oz. (600ml.) white latex flat paint / 3½ fl. oz. (100ml.) monestial blue artists' acrylic color / 3tbsp. medium gray artists' acrylic color (2 coats)
Sealant coat ▶ 12 fl. oz. (350ml.) furniture wax (clear)
Punching the tin ▶ tin-plated sheet steel for lower panels / 3½ fl. oz. (100ml.) paint thinner / 3½ fl. oz. (100ml.) beeswax polish / 7 fl. oz. (210ml.) strong-bonding, non-drip, multipurpose contact adhesive / 8 brass-headed nails
Frosting the glass ▶ 5 fl. oz. (150ml.) etch cream
Preparing the zinc ▶ sheet zinc for unit top
Fixing the zinc ▶ 4 fl. oz. (120ml.) strong-bonding, non-drip, multipurpose contact adhesive / approx. 30 copper roofing nails
Reassembling ▶ approx. 8 finishing nails / 2 chrome door handles / 2 chrome drawer pulls / screws (if not supplied) / small dowels (if required)

EQUIPMENT

Screwdriver / small chisel (if required, to remove putty) / newspaper / marker / metal rule / 2 containers for mixing paint / mixing sticks / 2 x 2in. (50mm.) latex brushes / 2 x 1in. (25mm.) round fitches / fine- and medium-grade sandpaper / lint-free cotton rags / ruler or straightedge / pencil / 1in. (2.5cm.) masking tape / china marker / tinsnips / rubber mallet / ½in. (12mm.) particleboard, approx. 1 x 2ft. (30 x 60cm.) / photocopier / 2 sheets tracing paper approx. 17 x 24in. (43 x 61cm.) / center punch / tack hammer / cotton gloves / waterproof sandpaper / brawdawl or drill with metal bit / gaffer tape (for unfitted glass) / scissors / window cleaner / 2 sheets appliqué film approx 8½ x 11in. (22 x 28cm.) / cutting mat / X-Acto knife / large plate / 1 x 1in. (25mm.) tossaway brush / 1 x 4in. (100mm.) sponge mini-roller / permanent pen / tile cutter / brick chisel / claw hammer / 2 x 2in. (50 x 50mm.) batten (to shape zinc), approx. 12in. (30cm.) / protective mask / pliers / coarse steel wool

FRENCH DRESSER

1 Remove all the handles, knobs, and hinges, using the screwdriver. Store the handles, knobs, and screws for possible future use. Spray the hinges with two coats of silver metallic paint, allowing 1 hour for each coat to dry, and set them aside for refixing later.

2 Using the tip of the screwdriver, very carefully loosen the nails in the battens that support the glass, and take out both pieces. A small chisel is a great help if you have to remove old putty—but be gentle.

3 Wrap sound glass in several sheets of newspaper and label clearly with the marker. Take measurements for new glass, if required. Set the battens aside for painting.

Aged paint finish

See page 144 for the technique. I applied the ice blue top coats over a creamy white. If you want a subtly aged effect (as here), apply the wax resist sparingly—just to the door edges and moldings.

Sealant coat

Using clean rags folded into a pad, apply the furniture wax, leave to set (15 minutes), and buff up.

Punching the tin

See page 177 for the technique; for the motifs, page 182. Our door panels each measure approx. 1 x 2ft (30.5 x 61cm.) (30.5 x 16cm).I added a line to follow the shape of each panel. To do the same, use a ruler to draw a line approx. ½in. (12mm.) from the edge of the tracing once you have transferred the motifs. Punch the marks for the decorative lines ⅜in. (1cm.) apart, but leave smaller gaps (approx. ¼in. [5mm.] when forming letters.

Frosting the glass

See page 180 for the technique and page 182 for the motif. Our glass panels were 11 x 18in. (28 x 46cm.). I used 1in. (2.5cm.) masking tape for the stripes above and below each cup, but they might look even better if I had used a narrower tape. Remember to reverse one of the cups when tracing the motifs so that both handles will face inward.

Preparing the zinc

1 Using the metal rule, ruler (or straightedge), and marker, make a pattern for the dresser worktop out of newspaper, adding allowances for all four edges, including turned-under widths at front and sides as shown on the sketch on page 182. Our top measured 17⅜ x 33½in. (44 x 85cm.).

2 Stick your pattern to the wrong side of the zinc sheet with masking tape, draw around the basic outline with the permanent pen, and cut out, using the tinsnips.

3 Again using the ruler, metal rule, and permanent pen, carefully transfer all the fold and cut lines from your pattern to the zinc. Accuracy will make folding much easier.

4 Using the tinsnips, make the small corner cut as shown in the diagram. This separates the turn-unders at the front from those at the side. Snip the other three corners in the same way.

5 Flatten the cut edges and protect with masking tape.

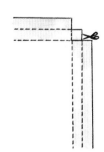

6 See Shaping and Bending a Zinc Sheet on page 25, step 1, line 5 onward, for the technique. The initial shaping (scoring and then marking with the brick chisel) is carried outt on the reverse side of the zinc. Turn the sheet over and position on the unit before you start to bend the fold at the back and the inner folds at the sides and front. Although this may seem an unneccessarily complicated process, that batten is important. If you hammer a zinc surface directly, you will mark it. You'll also find the batten helps you to spread the pressure as you work on the folds.

Fixing the zinc

1 Remove the zinc and, using medium-grade sandpaper, sand the unit top and the corresponding reverse section of zinc. Wipe clean with a damp rag; leave to dry.

2 Put on the protective mask, stir the glue well, and apply evenly to both surfaces with the fitch used to glue the tin.

3 Re-position the zinc on the unit top, and smooth the glued surface down, using the batten and hammer. (It takes approx. 25 minutes for the glue to dry.)

4 Working with the hammer and wood as before, continue shaping the back, front, and sides. Bend the outer sections at the sides and front under the overhangs.

5 To finish the corners, use the pliers to fold each corner tab in half diagonally, bending the top corner downward and backward (see Fig 1). Then, using the hammer and wood again, bend each triangular tab around its corner to the side. Hammer very gently to avoid creating sharp edges here.

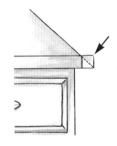

Fig. 1 Front view

6 Make a pilot hole with the brawdawl or metal bit, and secure each tab with a copper nail (see Fig 2). Four will secure the top; but if (like me) you want to feature the nails, tap in all around, spacing them evenly. These nails have long shafts, so shorten them with the tinsnips first.

7 Using the coarse steel wool and a circular action, rub the top down to improve the texture of the zinc—it is often sold covered with a waxy film. Wipe clean with a damp rag.

Reassembling

1 Slot the glass back into the door panels, and replace the battens, securing with finishing nails.

2 Screw the resprayed hinges back onto the unit, and rehang all the doors, using the original screws.

Fig. 2 Side view

3 Attach the new handles and drawer pulls, checking first that the original holes in the wood are the correct size for the screws supplied with the new fittings. If they are too small, use the bradawl or drill to enlarge them slightly. If too large, plug the holes with small dowels to fit.

4 Position the upper section carefully on top of the base.

GILDED TABLE

Round one-piece and gateleg dining tables are so commonplace in the secondhand shops I haunt, it's easy to overlook them. But some offer such excellent value to anyone furnishing a first home that it seemed feeble to resist the challenge they represent. Here, then, I concentrate on the cheaper end of the spectrum, avoiding hardwoods like oak and mahogany, which are best simply restored, and suggest one way of creating interest on a neglected space—the tabletop. It's an idea that could be adapted for tables of any shape or size.

GILDED TABLE

CLEANING AND PRIMING

Prepare the surface thoroughly by cleaning and priming as appropriate. See pages 12–17.

MATERIALS

Base coat ▶ 24 fl. oz. (710ml.) white latex flat paint / 10 fl. oz. (300ml.) monestial blue acrylic artists' color
Gilding base coat ▶ 12 fl. oz. (350ml.) deep blue latex flat paint
Size coat ▶ 12 fl. oz. (350ml.) water-based size
Gilding ▶ 40 loose sheets imitation gold (Dutch metal) leaf
Sealant coats ▶ 1 quart (1 liter) clear satin acrylic varnish (2 coats)

EQUIPMENT

Container for mixing paint / mixing sticks / 2 x 2in. (50mm.) latex brushes / pencil / ruler or straightedge / right-angled triangle / metal rule / small nail / tack hammer / newspaper and scissors for pattern (if required, see below) / approx. 1yd. (1m.) string / graph paper / plastic ruler and masking tape (optional) / disposable gloves / 1 x 1in. (25mm.) flat bristle brush / 1 x 1in. (25mm.) round, very soft-bristled brush or clean dustcloth / 1 x 2in. (50mm.) varnish brush

INSTRUCTIONS
Base coat

1 Pour the latex paint into the container. Add the monestial blue and stir well.
2 Apply two even coats to the entire table with one of the latex brushes. Allow 2–3 hours for each coat to dry.

Drawing the checkerboard

1 To find the center of your table, follow steps 2–3 or 4–5.
2 If it is a drop-leaf table, lower the flaps to form two straight sides. Using the pencil, ruler (or straightedge), and triangle, draw a line down each of the other two sides to complete a rectangle. Mark the halfway point on each long side, and rule a line between them.
3 Mark the halfway point of that line and you have found the center. Tap the nail lightly into the center point, and raise the table flaps. Ignore steps 4–5.
4 If it is not a drop-leaf table, tape several sheets of newspaper together, place the table upside down on them and draw around its circumference with the pencil. Cut out the resulting pattern, fold into quarters, and you have the center point.
5 Unfold the pattern, lay it on the table (right side up!), tap the nail lightly into the center, and remove the pattern.
6 Once your nail is in position, tie one end of the string to it to form the "fixed arm" of your improvised compass. Draw the string taut, and experiment to decide on the size of your circle. Mine had a diameter of 42½in. (107.5cm.). Trim the string, if necessary, and tie the pencil to the free end, making allowance for the knot. Carefully draw your circle.

7 Use the triangle and ruler to divide the circle into quarters, taking the line drawn through the center point as a guide. (If you used a pattern to find your center point, you need to draw this line first.) Then measure and draw a grid of equally spaced vertical and horizontal lines to create your checkerboard. Mine was based on a 5in. (12.5cm.) square—convenient because my Dutch metal leaves were this size—but rule your design out to scale on graph paper to check fit.

Gilding

For the technique, see page 168, including the Sealant coat. Gilding was applied to alternate squares of the checkerboard and the edge of the table on a base coat of deep blue. Use a plastic ruler (beveled side down) as a guide if you are worried about painting straight lines. It's your choice how much of the base coat shows, but subtlety works best.

Sealant coats

Stir the varnish well, and apply one or two coats to the entire table. Allow 2–3 hours for each coat to dry.

MASKING

This simple effect can add instant interest to any flat or textured surface. All you need is a quantity of flat shapes to mask the chosen areas. Try, as I did, looking for readymade masks. Experiment is the key word—with colors as well as shapes. You may choose to work with natural forms, but that's no reason to limit yourself to nature's hues. To secure your mask, spray a thin coat of spray adhesive on the reverse (except for ferns, see below) and press firmly into place. For the spray technique, see page 99. Cover the entire surface, including the masks, for an even finish, but avoid soaking paper. Peel off gently before the paint begins to dry. (See pages 42–3 for sealants.)

Below: Falling plane tree leaves inspired this effect, although I've never seen them so well behaved. I used more than fifty gathered in a local park—often a good hunting ground. Press in thick books first. Colorway: primer and base coat—see page 52; top coat—burgundy acrylic spray paint. Less formal patterns look good, too.

Above: Simple motifs with bold color contrasts work best for well-defined images, and a smooth surface may also sharpen an image. But if you opt for harmonizing color or the smudgy effect of spraying through complex patterns, the results are often delightful, as here. Colorway: white acrylic spray primer; base coat—oatmeal acrylic spray paint; top coat—deep blue acrylic spray paint. Masking with lace can be effective on smooth surfaces.

Some green ferns make wonderful masks. I begged mine from a friend, but florists sometimes hold a stock. Press and place face down—the underside is often dotted with tiny, dusty spores. It's wise to brush your surface before spraying, too.

Colorway: white acrylic spray primer; base coat—salmon pink acrylic spray paint; top coat—as cabinet opposite.

KITCHEN TABLE
TO CONSOLE TABLES

This is the kind of project that really pleases me. The end result is a handsome pair of narrow tables that would stand happily in a long hallway, in the alcoves on either side of a fireplace (instead of the ubiquitous bookshelves), or flanking a tall window. But they started life as one very plain, rectangular kitchen table topped with a laminate that was beginning to lift off. Don't let the construction deter you—it's pretty basic, and you can always enlist someone else's help if you prefer. My design and decoration were inspired at least partly by the Gothick Revival style of the late eighteenth century, though it's easy enough to reshape the backplate and leg insets in some very different style.

CLEANING AND PRIMING

Prepare the surface thoroughly by cleaning before and after construction and by priming. See pages 12–17.

MATERIALS

Preparation ▸ ⅜in. (9mm.) plywood or MDF
Construction ▸ 12 screws / ¾ x ¾in. (19 x 19mm.) quarter-round wood / 2 fl. oz. (60ml.) wood glue / 40 finishing nails / ½ x ½in. (12 x 12mm.) batten
Base coat ▸ 15 fl. oz. (440ml.) white latex flat paint / 2tbsp. raw umber artists' acrylic color / 2tbsp. burnt umber artists' acrylic color
Wax resist ▸ 3½ fl. oz. (100ml.) furniture wax (clear)
Top coat ▸ 1 pint (500ml.) premixed deep orange-red latex flat paint (1 coat only)
Aging glaze ▸ 5 fl. oz. (150ml.) acrylic glazing liquid (transparent) / 1tbsp. premixed deep orange-red latex flat paint / ½tbsp. burnt umber artists' acrylic color
Découpage ▸ photocopies as required / 3½ fl. oz. (100ml.) green water-based ink / 5tsp. water (to dilute) / 2 fl. oz. (60ml.) white glue
Aging wax ▸ 5 fl. oz. (150ml.) furniture wax (clear) / 1tsp. raw sienna artists' oil color
Fixing ▸ screws and wall fixings (see pages 27–8)

EQUIPMENT

Pencil / ruler or straightedge / right-angled triangle / adjustable workbench and/or C-clamps / protective mask (if using MDF) / jigsaw / medium- and fine-grade sandpaper / metal rule / photocopier / paper approx. 17 x 24in. (43 x 61cm.) / scissors / drill with wood and masonry bits / screwdriver / backsaw / 1 x ½in. (12mm.) round fitch / tack hammer / 2 containers for mixing paint and glaze / mixing sticks / 3 x 2in. (50mm.) latex brushes / 1 x 1in. (25mm.) round fitch / lint-free cotton rags / small artists' brush / 3 saucers / cotton swabs / natural sponge / newspaper to protect work surface / 1 x 1in. (25mm.) tossaway brush

KITCHEN TABLE TO CONSOLE TABLES

INSTRUCTIONS

ALWAYS WEAR A MASK IF CUTTING MDF.

Preparation

1 Mark the cut line clearly across the tabletop, using the pencil, ruler (or straightedge), and right-angled triangle. Our table was divided in half to make two pieces 11½in.

(29.5cm.) deep and 35¾in. (91cm.) wide. If the table you plan to use is larger, or you want narrower consoles, you may need to draw two cut lines to the desired depth. (The central section will be thrown away once the table is cut.)

2 Secure the table with C-clamps to keep it steady, and cut along the pencil line with the jigsaw. Rub the cut edges with sandpaper until they are smooth.

3 Measure the width (or cut edge) of one of the tabletops and, using a photocopier and the large sheets of paper, enlarge the template for the backplate on page 183 to fit. Enlarge the template for the leg insets to the appropriate size.

4 Cut out the full-sized templates, and check the backplate against your table. You may need to adapt the lower section to secure it to your base. Now is also the time to consider making adjustments to the upper section. You can use newspaper to patch the existing template or even recut it to create a different profile. Hold your revised template in position to check its proportions.

5 Once you are happy with the backplate, lay the templates on the wood—we used a piece of MDF approx. 39 x 39in. (1 x 1m.)—and draw a clear line around them. You need two backplates and four leg insets for a pair of tables.

6 Clamp the wood securely, and cut out the pieces, using the jigsaw. Smooth the cut edges with sandpaper.

Construction

1 Turn one table to lie cut edge upward, and ask someone to hold one of the backplates in place while you mark with the pencil the positions of the six screws that will join it to the table. You need four along the cut edge of the tabletop and one below at each side to secure it to the base.

2 With the backplate still held firmly in position, drill the six screw holes, making sure the drill passes through the backplate and into the table.

3 Using the screwdriver, join the backplate to the table.

4 Turn the table over and, using the backsaw, cut a piece of quarter-round to the width of the table. This will finish the join between the tabletop and backplate.

5 Using the small fitch, brush a narrow strip of wood glue onto the tabletop where the batten will sit. Position the batten and secure by tapping in four finishing nails, using the tack hammer.

6 Turn the table upside down and place one of the leg insets in position. Tap a finishing nail into the table base and another into the leg to secure it temporarily. Repeat for the other leg.

7 To support and strengthen the insets, cut four pieces of square batten to match the straight sides of the design—we needed two long and two short ones, in total approx. 3ft. (1m.).

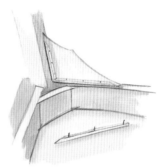

8 Using a pair of pieces for each inset, glue the battens to the inside of the inset, table base, and leg. Tap three finishing nails into each piece to secure. (We decided to tap the finishing nails partway into the battens before brushing on the glue. There was less risk of disturbing the insets when securing them.) Allow all glued areas to dry before painting (1 hour).

9 Repeat steps 1–8 to assemble the other table.

Aged paint finishes	See page 144, Wax-Resist method, and page 147, Aging with Glaze. I used a specially mixed cream base coat under a single top coat of premixed deep orange-red latex flat for the resist technique. The burnt umber in the aging glaze darkens the red top coat to add a convincing patina. I delayed a sealant coat (see Aging wax, below) until I had added the découpage.
Découpage	See page 161, Tinting with Water-based Inks, and the Basic Recipe. I colored all the photocopies with a diluted green ink. (Ignore the base and sealant coats.)
Aging wax	See page 146. Tinted with raw sienna, this gives a softer, aged look to the découpage and paint finish.
Fixing to the wall	Fit the masonry bit to the drill, and ask someone to hold each table in position while you drill two holes through the lower section of the backplate and into the wall. Secure as appropriate (see pages 27–8).

CAFÉ TABLES

The simple design of the café table is a classic, but if the one you have is a little battered, you'd like a change, or you just want to jazz up your garden with a new look for a long-running standard, any of these ideas would work well. Each one offers a resilient finish suitable for outdoor use, but each is also attractive enough for a sunroom or garden room and other informal indoor uses. Just substitute two coats of polyurethane varnish for the marine varnish mentioned on pages 86–7.

Although I concentrate on the tabletop here, the legs can also be decorated in a variety of finishes, such as verdigris, gilding, or bronzing (see pages 166–9), and you could decorate the accompanying chairs with a similar or complementary finish for a stunning addition to your garden. If you want to try but don't have a metal café table, check out the large chain stores for inexpensive copies—a cheaper and better option than chasing the limited supply of secondhand originals. You can adapt these ideas for wooden or plastic laminate tabletops, too. Or, on a grander scale for high days and holidays, have a much larger circle cut from particleboard, and support it on inexpensive trestles.

MOSAIC TABLE TOP

CLEANING/PRIMING

Prepare the surface by cleaning and priming. See pages 12–17.

MATERIALS

Preparation ▶ tiles (all ¾ x ¾in. [19 x 19mm.])—approx. 225 pale blue / 225 pale green / 450 ultramarine / 150 orange / 150 red / 150 yellow / 100 black / 100 assorted gold and turquoise
Fixing the tiles ▶ 1 pint (500ml.) clear, strong PVA glue
Grouting the tiles ▶ 1 pint (500ml.) ceramic tile grout
Tinting the grout ▶ 2tsp. pale olive green artists' acrylic color / 1tsp. titanium white artists' acrylic color / 5tsp. water

EQUIPMENT

See page 174, omitting ruler and photocopier and adding compass with extendable arm.

INSTRUCTIONS

See page 174. There's no need to buy a compass. Just improvise by drawing around several plates to create the circles which are the basis of this essentially simple design. You can vary the sizes, but remember that any changes you make will have an effect on color quantities. I laid the tiles approx. ⅟₁₆–⅛in. (2–3mm.) apart.

CAFÉ TABLES

STAMPED TABLETOP

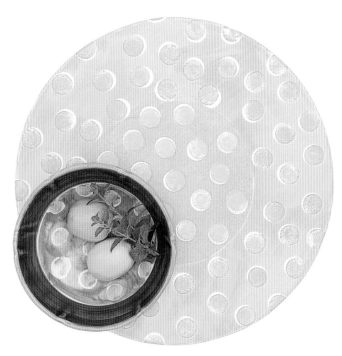

CLEANING/PRIMING Prepare the surface by cleaning and priming. See pages 12–17.

MATERIALS Base coat (outer circle) ▶ 10 fl. oz. (300ml.) deep yellow latex flat paint
Top coat (outer circle) ▶ 4tsp. cadmium yellow artists' acrylic color / 2tsp. titanium white artists' acrylic color
Base coat (inner circle) ▶ 5 fl. oz. (150ml.) white latex flat paint / 4 fl. oz. (120ml.) cobalt blue artists' acrylic color / 5tsp. emerald green acrylic
Top coat (inner circle) ▶ 5tsp. permanent light blue (phthalocyanine blue) artists' acrylic color
Stamping the dots ▶ 8tbsp. titanium white artists' acrylic color / 4tbsp. permanent light blue (phthalocyanine blue) artists' acrylic color / 4tbsp. brilliant yellow-green artists' acrylic color
Sealant coats ▶ 25 fl. oz. (740ml.) clear matte marine varnish (3 coats)

EQUIPMENT Compass or large plate / pencil / ruler / 1 sheet appliqué film 17 x 24in. (43 x 61cm.) / X-Acto knife / cutting mat / 2 x 1½in. (38mm.) latex brushes / 5 saucers / 2 x 2in. (50mm.) latex brushes / 3 x 1⅜in. (35mm.) diameter sponges for mini-roller / 1 x 2in. (50mm.) varnish brush

INSTRUCTIONS See page 31 for how to use appliqué film. Draw a circle with a diameter of 10½in. (27cm) on the film and cut it out, keeping both pieces. Mask the center of the table with the circle and apply the base coat to the outer circle, allowing to dry (2–3 hours). Dip just the brush tip into the top coat color-mix to dry brush the outer circle. Repeat for the inner circle using the other mask. See page 164 for stamping.

LAPIS LAZULI TABLETOP

For a straight take on the technique shown on page 154, just double the quantities given. Equipment and instructions are as there. But hold the fitch 8–12in. (20–30cm) from the surface while you spatter, and prepare the surface first (see pages 12–17). For sealant coats, see opposite.

DÉCOUPAGE TABLETOP

See page 161, Tinting with Water-based Inks, for the technique. I used 5 oz (150ml) bright green ink to tint the paper. The base coat (1 pint [500ml] white latex flat paint mixed with 31/3tbsp dioxazine purple artists' acrylic color) was dry brushed (see opposite) with a mix of 5 oz (150ml) acrylic glazing liquid and 2tsp. dioxazine purple. For Cleaning and Priming, see pages 12–17. For sealant coats, see opposite.

LAMINATED
KITCHEN UNITS

There's no need to despair of dragging those old kitchen units into the twenty-first century. Car spray paint and judicious restyling of knobs and pulls will render the uggliest melamine-coated fixtures unrecognizable. Try out paints before committing to a color scheme.

CLEANING AND PRIMING

Prepare the surface thoroughly by cleaning; prime with white acrylic spray primer. See pages 12–17; see also page 99 for spray technique.

MATERIALS

Preparation ▶ 1in. (25mm.) plywood for worktop, precut to size (see page 90) Frames, drawer fronts, and doors ▶ (for base unit: 34½ x 42in. [88 x 107cm.]; upper unit: 28 x 38in. [71 x 97cm.] / 10 fl. oz. (300ml.) copper metallic car spray paint / 13½ fl. oz. (400ml.) deep purple acrylic spray paint / 13½ fl. oz. (400ml.) mint green acrylic spray paint / 10 fl. oz. (300ml.) pale blue metallic car spray paint / 5 fl. oz. (150ml.) peach metallic car spray paint Sealant coats ▶ 1¼ quarts (1.2 liters) clear satin acrylic spray varnish (2 coats) Final assembly ▶ 1in. (2.5cm.) self-stick, chrome trim or fake leading / 6 chrome knobs with appropriate screws

EQUIPMENT

Screwdriver / metal rule / drop cloths / 1 x 4in. (10cm.) roll brown-paper painter's tape / scissors / protective mask / 4 sheets appliqué film approx. 12 x 16½in. (30 x 42cm.) / compass with extendable arm or large plate or similar / pencil / cutting mat / X-Acto knife / right-angled triangle / ruler or straightedge / knife with rounded handle / drill with wood bit (if required)

INSTRUCTIONS
Preparation

PROTECT YOUR WORK SPACE WITH PLASTIC DROP CLOTHS BEFORE SPRAYING, WORK IN A WELL-VENTILATED AREA, AND WEAR A MASK.

1 Take out the drawers and use an appropriate screwdriver to remove all the doors. Store screws—for use later.
2 Remove any handles; it's so much easier to achieve good, even coverage when spraying without them.

3 Carefully remove the worktop from the base unit, noting how and where it is attached. Store the brackets and screws for later use.

4 Measure the length and width of the worktop before disposing of it. Ask your lumberyard to cut the new plywood top to the correct size. Ours was 42 x 20¾in. (107 x 53cm.).

Spraying the unit frames and drawers

With the same spray technique (see Priming) and brown-paper painter's tape to prevent overspill, use copper for the plinth and purple for the remainder of the base unit, spraying the outside only. See page 31 for the masking technique. No masking is needed when spraying the upper unit mint green or the drawers copper—again outsides only.

Spraying the upper doors

1 For the outside of the left-hand door, use self-stick appliqué film to prevent overspill when spraying the circle blue and the remainder of the door peach. See pages 31 for the masking technique. If you don't already own an extendable compass, don't buy one specially. The easiest and cheapest solution is to improvise with a large plate or even a pie pan of the right diameter. Place it on the appliqué film, draw around it with the pencil, and your problem is solved. My circle had a 13½in. (34cm.) diameter.

2 For the outside of the right-hand door, mask with brown paper to spray a copper rectangle and mint green frame. My rectangle was approx. 10 x 18in. (25 x 46cm.).

Spraying the base doors

1 For the outside of the left-hand door, use two strips of evenly spaced 4in. (10cm.) brown-paper painter's tape to spray alternate stripes of mint green and copper. Check the positions of the tape with the metal rule, ruler (or straightedge), and triangle before spraying.

2 For the outside of the right-hand door, see Spraying the upper doors, step 1—but reverse the colors, making the circle peach this time.

Sealant coats

Shake the varnish well, and apply two coats to all the sprayed surfaces and to the worktop, allowing 1 hour between coats and 2–3 hours for the second coat to dry.

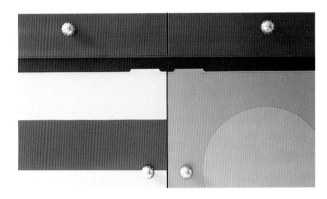

Final assembly

1 Position the varnished worktop and secure in the same way as before, using all the original brackets and screws.

2 To add the chrome trim or fake leading, measure the edges you want to cover, and cut the required length(s), using the scissors. I decided to cover the front and both sides of ours.

3 Peel off the backing and press the trim or leading in place, smoothing it with the handle of the knife. Work on small sections at a time. See the illustration on page 21.

4 Where necessary, drill a screw hole for the new handle in each of the doors and attach, using the screws provided. Repeat for the drawers.

5 Replace doors, using original screws.

SPRAYING FRIDGES AND FREEZERS

You can use the same spraying and masking techniques to brighten these dreary monoliths, too. So here are just a few, probably unnecessary, reminders. Empty, disconnect, and defrost (if necessary) before you begin! Wash down with a de-greaser solution. Use masking tape and/or painter's tape to protect all switches, knobs, door handles, and seals. Don't attempt to remove the handles or spray the "working" parts at the back. Handles make it more difficult to achieve a smooth finish, but you may damage the machine if you take them off. Keep the door(s) closed while spraying; open to dry.

For this fridge-freezer (which was approx. 23 x 72in. (58.5 x 183cm.), I primed with 27 fl. oz. (800ml.) gray acrylic spray primer, decorated with 1¼ quarts (1.2 liters) silver acrylic spray paint and 13 fl. oz. (380ml.) blue metallic car spray paint, and added a sealant coat of clear lacquer spray (13 fl. oz. [380ml.]), allowing 1–2 hours for that to dry.

METAL

The real fun of using paint finishes that look like metal is the element of surprise you can introduce to almost any interior. The kitchen cabinet apparently fashioned of beaten copper and the verdigris chair both come into that category, and I have seen a stunning metal effect on a sixties sideboard. Simple forms—hard-edged shapes that could be made of metal—will almost always help you create convincing results; and this might be the solution if you are tired of the sleek, matte black laminate look that dominated eighties interiors. Verdigris and copper effects can also work well with more rounded, wrought forms. The traditional bentwood chair is one obvious example—inexpensive copies are not hard to find. You can use these finishes on real metal, too, of course; and with new filing cabinets fairly expensive, this is a great way of brightening old equipment for a home office. See page 166 for the paint techniques and pages 42–3 for sealants. The "studs" mentioned in the captions are upholstery nails, tapped in before priming.

Pewter for a bedside cabinet: the slightly pitted surface of black laminate on chipboard took spray paint well and contributed to the final result. This is the low-key partner in my trio of metal effects, so I opted for funky new handles (made of plastic) and sprayed them copper. Note the discreet stud on each side.

Right: A copper effect gives this tired kitchen cabinet a space-age feel. Studs, placed approx. 3in (7.5cm) apart, frame the doors and inscribe two centered circles. The dark halo effect was pure serendipity. One coat of primer had failed to hide an earlier paint finish, but I liked the look so much that I emphasized it when applying the glaze. New plastic handles sprayed silver add that final lift.

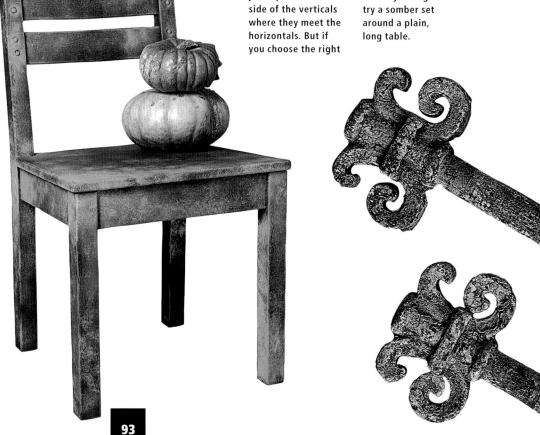

Left: This chain-store chair is almost medieval, given a verdigris finish. I wish I'd used studs on the legs, too— just a pair on each side of the verticals where they meet the horizontals. But if you choose the right setting, the effect will still convince. A single chair in a hallway could look great—and if you have a sense of drama you might try a somber set around a plain, long table.

NO-SEW COVER
FOR AN OLD SOFA

If your sofa is showing its age, but you can't afford to buy a new one, why not make a cover for it? This needn't involve vast amounts of cutting, fitting, and stitching. Our solution takes the conventional approach, a throw, one step further by using a cotton drop cloth, which must be some of the cheapest fabric around; and it deals with the disadvantage of throws—they just don't stay put. Using diaper pins, a few buttons, and (in the case of the chair shown on page 97) stout rubber bands, these covers will survive the heaviest video session.

MATERIALS

**Dyeing ▶ 1 new cotton drop cloth (approx. 3⅔ x 3⅔yd. [3.3 x 3.3m.]) / detergent / 7 oz. (200g.) yellow cold-wash hand dye / water according to the manufacturer's instructions / 1 lb. (500g.) salt
Preparing the pins ▶ 54 diaper pins or other large safety pins / 3½fl. oz. (100ml.) yellow fast-drying enamel spray paint
Covering the sofa ▶ 108 small green beads / 108 small red beads / 4 red buttons / red thread / 3 green buttons / green thread**

EQUIPMENT

Washing machine / plastic drop cloth / rubber gloves / plastic garbage bin or other large container for dyeing / mixing stick / iron / masking tape / scissors / approx. 1 in. (2.5cm.) polystyrene foam (12in.2/[30 cm.2]) / protective mask / semicircular upholstery repair needle or ordinary needle

INSTRUCTIONS
Dyeing

PROTECT YOUR WORK SPACE WITH DROP CLOTHS BEFORE SPRAYING, WORK IN A WELL-VENTILATED AREA, AND WEAR A MASK.

1 Machine wash the cotton drop cloth five times, using your usual detergent, and hang to dry naturally. This sounds laborious, I know; but learn from my mistakes. First, it takes that many washes to remove all traces of the manufacturer's finish, which is essential if the dye is to take evenly. Second, if you tumble dry this fabric it will shrink.

2 Protect your work space with the plastic drop cloth and your hands with rubber gloves. Following the manufacturer's instructions, make up the cold-water dye in a container large enough to take dye and fabric. I used a plastic garbage bin, checked first for leaks and scrubbed thoroughly!

3 Again following the instructions, dye the fabric, rinse until the water is clear, wring out, and hang to dry naturally.

4 Press, using a medium-hot iron.

Preparing the pins

1 Open each diaper pin, cover the metal sections with masking tape and stick into the polystyrene foam.

2 Shake the spray can well, and apply two thin, even coats to the plastic parts of the pins with steady, sweeping strokes, allowing 1 hour for each coat to dry.

Covering the sofa

1 Lay the fabric over the sofa, draping it to conceal the original upholstery. Tuck in a little fabric at the back and sides of the seat where necessary, and work out the natural folding places at each side, front, and back. Arrange the fabric at the folds to form an inverted pleat.

2 Working from top to bottom and beginning just below seat level at the inner arm, use diaper pins to secure the pleat on each side at the front. Thread each pin with one green and one red bead, push the point through the folds of the pleat, and then thread another red bead and green bead before fastening.

3 Repeat the process to secure the pleat at each side at the back. These will be longer, so, again starting from the top, use twenty pins for each side.

4 To secure the fabric on the arms, use the needle and thread to sew two evenly spaced buttons, one red and one green, halfway up each inside arm. You need to push the needle through the fabric and into the upholstery each time before drawing it out again—the special semicircular upholsterers' needle I recommend makes the job very easy, but it's not difficult with an ordinary needle. To remove the cover for washing is simplicity itself—just undo the pins and cut through the button threads.

5 To secure the fabric at the front below the seat, sew on three evenly spaced buttons in the same way: a green button in the middle and a red one on either side.

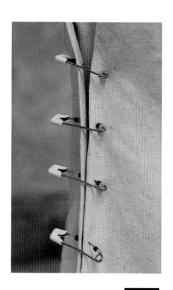

COVERING A LOW CHAIR

MATERIALS

Dyeing the fabric ▶ ½ new cotton drop cloth or similar fabric (approx. 1⅘ x 1⅘yd. [1.65 x 1.65m.]), plus half quantities listed for Sofa Covering the chair ▶ 4 large thick rubber bands / approx 13ft. (12m.) ribbon in three colors (dark green, medium blue, and lavender) / 7 buttons / matching thread

EQUIPMENT

As Sofa, but omit masking tape, foam, and mask, and add sewing machine

INSTRUCTIONS
Dyeing

Follow the instructions for the Sofa. Turn and machine stitch the raw edges, and press again.

Covering the chair

1 Lay the fabric over the chair, concealing the upholstery and legs completely, and tuck in a little fabric at the back of the seat.

2 Working on the front of the seat first, use both hands to gather the excess cloth into two equal bunches, one at each side, and secure with rubber bands.

3 Form another two bunches at the back of the seat—one at either side—just above the point where seat and back meet. Check and adjust the drapery to your taste. It is best to keep the fullness at the sides so that front and back are uncluttered.

4 Cut the three ribbons into varying lengths. Take one piece of each color and twist them around one of the front bunches, concealing the rubber band and leaving loose ends of different lengths. Repeat for the other front bunch. Vary the colors for the sides, tying some of the ends to form a bow.

5 To secure the fabric at the front, just below the seat, sew on three buttons, spacing them evenly and using the method described in Covering the sofa, step 4.

6 Secure the fabric at the sides in the same way. I used one button at each side of the seat and another high on the sides of the back.

THREE WAYS WITH
A DINING CHAIR

It's easy enough to pick up cheap, sturdy, upright chairs in junk shops, though singletons are more common than sets. That hardly matters if you pick a color (or colors) and paint finish to unite them. In these three projects I've selected standard designs dating from the last thirty or forty years and given them a variety of simple treatments, traditional and contemporary, which could be applied to any number of other chairs. If my way with lift-out seats persuades you to reconsider the potential in some ponderous set of forties castoffs with lumpy legs, I'll be happy. Remember, too, that in small households where space and money are limited, one of the advantages of harmonizing, multicolored sets of dining chairs is that they can be dual function—serving time in a bedroom or bathroom and pressed into service only when guests arrive. All that needs is careful color coordination.

MACHINE-AGE METALLIC

CLEANING AND PRIMING

Remove lift-out seat and set aside for covering. Prepare the surface thoroughly by cleaning; prime with white acrylic spray primer. See pages 12-17; see also below for spray technique.

Opposite (left to right): Peach, purple, and pale spearmint green top coats for a trio of sprayed chairs.

MATERIALS for one chair (right)

Top coat ▶ 10 fl. oz. (300ml.) peach metallic car spray paint
Sealant coats ▶ 10 fl. oz. (300ml.) clear satin acrylic spray varnish (2 coats)
Re-covering seat ▶ 18 x 18in. (0.5 x 0.5m.) pale blue upholstery velvet

EQUIPMENT

Drop cloths / protective mask / hand-held staple gun and staples / scissors

INSTRUCTIONS Top coat

Protect work space with drop cloths before spraying, work in a well-ventilated area; wear a mask. Shake the can well and spray with steady, sweeping strokes, holding the can 12in. (30.5cm.) from the prepared and primed surface. Aim for even coverage. Allow to dry (1 hour).

Sealant coats

Spray two even coats of varnish in the same way. Allow 1 hour for the first coat to dry, 2–3 hours for the second.

THREE WAYS WITH A DINING CHAIR

Re-covering the lift-out seat

1 If the seat fits only one way into its space, lay the square of velvet on top of it to decide which way you want the pile to lie. (Velvet has a light and a dark tone, depending on how light strikes the pile.) This is important if you are covering several seats with one color, unless you like the idea of using different tones.

2 Place the fabric right side down on a flat surface, and center the lift-out seat, topside down, on it.

3 Taking one edge at a time, fold the fabric over onto the underside of the seat and draw it taut. Staple to secure, placing a line of staples approx. 1in. (2.5cm.) from the edge. Repeat on the remaining three edges. This step is much easier if you can enlist another pair of hands.

4 Use the scissors to trim away the excess fabric, taking care not to cut too close to the staples.

RUSH SEAT FROM ARLES

CLEANING AND PRIMING

Prepare the surface thoroughly by cleaning; prime only the wood. See pages 12–17.

Fabric paints on artists' duck canvas for a sunflower cushion: use a dabbing action and don't overload your brush. Iron to seal.

MATERIALS

Base coats (wood) ▶ 1 pint (500ml.) premixed orange latex flat paint (2 coats)
Glaze coat (wood and rush) ▶ 8½ fl. oz. (250ml.) acrylic glazing liquid (transparent) / 3½ fl. oz. (100ml.) vermilion artists' acrylic color / 3⅓ tbsp. cadmium red artists' acrylic color
Sealant coat ▶ 8½ fl. oz. (250ml.) acrylic varnishing wax (clear)

EQUIPMENT

Mixing sticks / 2 x 2in. (50mm.) latex brushes / container for mixing glaze / lint-free cotton rags

INSTRUCTIONS Colorwashing (wood)

See page 152, basic recipe, for the technique. Set approx. a quarter of the glaze aside to dye the rushes.

Dyeing the rushes

See page 172, steps 2–3, for the technique. I used the same brush as for the wood, glaze top side only.

Sealant coat

With a clean rag, apply a thin, even coat of wax to the entire chair, wood and rush, working it in the direction of the weave. Allow to set (1 hour), and then buff with another rag.

FIFTIES RETRO

CLEANING AND PRIMING

Remove the lift-out seat and set aside for re-covering. Prepare the surface thoroughly by cleaning. See pages 12–17.

MATERIALS

Base coats ▶ 1 pint (500ml.) matte black paint (2 coats)
Glaze coat ▶ 3tbsp. acrylic glazing liquid (transparent) / 1tbsp. Mars black artists' acrylic color / 1tbsp. Titian buff artists' acrylic color
Sealant coat ▶ 8½fl. oz. (250ml.) acrylic varnishing wax (clear)
Re-covering the seat ▶ 18 x 18in. (0.5 x 0.5m.) white matte-finish vinyl for shower curtains and tables / 3tbsp. black fast-drying enamel paint

EQUIPMENT

Mixing sticks / 1 x 2in. (50mm.) tossaway brush / container for mixing glaze / 1 x 2in. (50mm.) latex brush / lint-free cotton rags / hand-held staple gun and appropriate staples / scissors / small, flat artists' brush

INSTRUCTIONS
Base coats

Stir the matte black paint well, and apply two coats to the prepared surface with the tossaway brush, allowing 3–4 hours for each coat to dry.

Glaze coat

1 Pour the glazing liquid into the container, add the Mars black and Titian buff, and stir well.
2 Dipping just the tip of the latex brush into the glaze, lightly brush the surface in the direction of the grain. Allow to dry (1–2 hours).

Sealant coat

See Rush Seat.

Re-covering the lift-out seat

1 See opposite, steps 2–4.
2 Stir the black enamel paint well, and, turning the seat right side up, use the flat artists' brush to decorate it with random long wavy lines. Allow to dry (1 hour) and replace.

A pad on the back can change a chair's profile as well as offering greater comfort. This one is secured with Velcro and took the same amount of vinyl as the seat. A slipcover minus padding, would change the look, too.

GIVERNY CHAIR

This is another of my favorite projects, yet it could hardly be simpler. The colorway, which owes more than a little to thoughts of Claude Monet's retreat at Giverny, cheers me up every time I look at it. The chair itself was stained black when I found it, and it must have started life as a sixties dining or kitchen chair, but it's now so scrumptious it would be a shame to hide most of it under some tabletop. Special pleading aside, what it usefully demonstrates is that some conventional surface like a chair can offer almost infinite opportunity to the imaginative. There's no rule stating that chairs must be just one color. I've seen successful pieces that take the notion much further than this. So go on, have fun!

Monet's water lilies also inspired the painted cushion. See the caption on page 100 for the basic method. Vary the size and shape of your brushes, and don't wash them too often—it helps the colors merge.

CLEANING AND PRIMING	**Prepare the surface thoroughly by cleaning and priming as appropriate. See pages 12–17.**
MATERIALS	**Base coats (seat and shoulder rest) ▶ 6 fl. oz. (180ml.) white latex flat paint / 3⅓tbsp. turquoise artists' acrylic color / 5tsp. monestial green artists' acrylic color (2 coats)** **Base coats (legs and rungs) ▶ 6 fl. oz. (180ml.) white latex flat paint / 5tbsp. permanent rose artists' acrylic color (2 coats)** **Wax resist ▶ 3½ fl. oz. (100ml.) furniture wax** **Top coats (seat and shoulder rest) ▶ see Base coat for the legs and rungs (2 coats)** **Top coats (legs and rungs) ▶ see Base coat for the seat and shoulder rest (2 coats)** **Sealant coat ▶ 8½ fl. oz. (250ml.) acrylic varnishing wax (clear)**
EQUIPMENT	**2 containers for mixing paint / mixing sticks / 2 x 2in. (50mm.) latex brushes / 1 x 1in. (25mm.) round fitch / small, flat artists' brush / fine-grade sandpaper / lint-free cotton rags**
INSTRUCTIONS **Aged paint finish**	See page 144, Wax Resist, for the technique. On the seat and shoulder rest I used aqua under pink, reversing the colorway for the legs and the rungs of the back. I added the pink rings on the rungs with the artists' brush after distressing, but they'd look better still if done before. Allow to dry (1–2 hours).
Sealant coat	Using clean rags folded into a pad, apply the varnishing wax, leave to set (15 minutes), and buff up with another clean rag.

TARTAN

If you thought tartan decoration was strictly for shortbread boxes, think again. Find the right harmonizing or contrasting color combinations, and you have a pattern to put a smile back on the saddest saleroom reject. The basic principles are explained on page 162. You needn't be limited by the size of the rollers available; some of the narrow stripes on these projects were hand painted, using low-tack masking tape to protect adjacent surfaces. Paint away from the tape to prevent "bleeding," and remove gently before the paint begins to dry.

NOTE In all three projects: "white" and "premixed" refer to latex flat paint; all other colors are artists' acrylics. Each was prepared and painted with white acrylic primer and protected with sealant (see pages 12–17 and 42–3).

Left: Here the verticals are set close. Colorway: base coat— 14 oz (410ml) white, 4tbsp. dioxazine purple; 1st grid—4 oz (120ml) white, 6½tbsp dioxazine purple, 2tbsp deep purple; gray horizontal stripe— 3½ oz (100ml) white, 3½ oz (100ml) medium gray; 2nd grid— 4tbsp white, 2tbsp oxide of chromium green.

Above: This strict pattern with a generous eye for color needs room to flaunt its complexities. Note how I've wrapped it over the sides—much more dynamic than centering. Colorway: base coat—premixed deep terracotta; legs and 1st grid —premixed deep blue; 2nd grid— (green stripe) 2⅓tbsp white, 2⅓tbsp oxide of chromium green, (purple stripe) 3½oz (100ml) white, 3½tbsp dioxazine purple; 3rd grid (liners)— use remains of 2nd.

A budget-store pine chest gets sunny style. Colorway: see page 163.

DECORATED
WOVEN CHAIRS

If you find a loom-woven chair in a junk shop or are lucky enough to inherit one, check what it's made of before attacking it with a paintbrush. The original Lloyd Loom chairs are much sought after and, sadly, once repainted, cannot be stripped because they were woven of paper, wrapped around wire. However, these chairs have become so popular in recent years that it is easy to find copies or updates of the styles first created in the twenties and thirties. My stencil designs have a soft period feel which suits the chairs admirably and can be applied either with sprays or with a brush. Unless your chair has already been heavily painted, I recommend spray for the top coat.

PEAR MOTIF—USING SPRAYS

CLEANING AND PRIMING

Clean the surface; prime with white acrylic spray primer. See pages 12–17; also page 99.

MATERIALS

Top coat ▶ 27 fl. oz. (800ml.) antique white acrylic spray paint
Stenciling ▶ 7 fl. oz. (210ml.) mint green acrylic spray paint / 7 fl. oz. (210ml.) moss green acrylic spray paint
Sealant coat ▶ 27 fl. oz. (800ml.) satin acrylic spray varnish

EQUIPMENT

Drop cloths / protective mask / photocopier / stencil paper / 16 x 16in. (40 x 40cm.) / masking tape / X-Acto knife / cutting mat / newspaper / cotton rags

INSTRUCTIONS
Top coat

PROTECT YOUR WORK SPACE WITH DROP CLOTHS BEFORE SPRAYING, WORK IN A WELL-VENTILATED AREA, AND WEAR A MASK.
Using the same spray technique (see Priming), apply an even coat of antique white and allow to dry (1 hour).

Stenciling

See page 157, Spraying, for the technique of cutting and using a stencil, and page 183 for the motif. I applied it randomly all over the chair, using mint green for the pears and the darker, moss green for the leaves and carefully adding a little moss green on one side of the pears to create shading.

Sealant coat

Spray a good, even coat of varnish over the entire chair. Allow to dry (1–2 hours).

Page 106: The Rose Motif is a hybrid. The primer (see Pear Motif), the top coat (27 oz [800ml] pink acrylic spray paint), and the sealant were all sprayed, but the stencils were stippled. Stencil colorway: light pink —3½ oz (100ml) white latex flat paint, 3½tbsp permanent rose acrylic color; dark pink—3½tbsp white latex flat paint, 2½tbsp permanent rose acrylic color; green—3½ oz (100ml) emerald green acrylic color, 3½tbsp white latex flat paint; sealant— see Pear Motif. For motif see page 183

PEACH MOTIF—USING BRUSHES

CLEANING/ PRIMING

Clean the surface; prime with white acrylic primer. See pages 12–17.

MATERIALS

Top coat ▶ 13½ fl. oz. (400ml.) white latex flat paint / 3½ fl. oz. (100ml.) cobalt blue artists' acrylic color
Stencils ▶ 7 fl. oz. (210ml.) white latex flat paint / 5 fl. oz. (150ml.) cadmium orange artists' acrylic color / 3½ fl. oz. (100ml.) pale olive green artists' acrylic color
Sealant coat ▶ 27 fl. oz. (800ml.) satin acrylic spray varnish

EQUIPMENT

See Pear Motif—omitting newspaper and substituting smaller stencil paper (9 x 9in. [23 x 23cm.]), plus container for mixing paint / mixing sticks / 1 x 2in. (50mm.) latex brush / 3 saucers / 3 x 1in. (25mm.) round stencil brushes

INSTRUCTIONS
Top coat

1 Pour the white latex paint into the container, add the cobalt blue, and mix well.

2 Apply evenly to the surface with the latex brush and allow to dry (1–2 hours).

Left: Peach Motif stencil colorway: light orange—3½ oz (100ml) white latex flat paint, 31/3tbsp cadmium orange acrylic color; dark orange—3½ oz (100ml) cadmium orange acrylic color, 3½ tbsp white latex flat paint; green—3½ oz (100ml) pale olive green acrylic color, 3½tbsp. white latex flat paint.

Stenciling

See page 159, Stippling, for the technique, and page 183 for the motif. Here I used the paler peach tone over the whole fruit, then, with the second stencil brush, stippled one side with darker peach for shaping and shading. The third brush was used for the green leaves. See caption for color mixes.

Sealant coat

See Pear Motif and follow the safety instructions. I decided to spray—it's so much easier to achieve a good finish on this surface.

THREE WAYS WITH
A METAL TRUNK

These three trunks were liberated from an aunt who'd discovered twelve of assorted sizes in an attic room when she moved into a new house several years ago. Dual function is the theme here—striking and attractive storage space plus some comfortable, but probably temporary seating. The scenario is yours to explore, but I've come up with three very different looks which could find a place in a variety of spaces—from an elegant hallway to a teenager's bedroom. Alternatively, adopt the seating idea but research naval or folk decoration for a period piece. Just one word of warning. As with the woven chairs, consider your trunk carefully before you begin, and if it already has real character or period interest, get advice before trying to change or restore it.

VERDIGRIS ANCESTRAL

CLEANING AND PRIMING

Prepare the surface thoroughly by cleaning; prime the inside of lid and entire outside with two coats of gray metal primer. See pages 12–17.

MATERIALS

**Preparation ▶ 1 x 2in. (25 x 50mm.) battens / ¾in. (19mm.) MDF or plywood
Construction ▶ 10 dome-headed brass screws
Base coats ▶ 1 pint (500ml.) matte black paint (2 coats)
Glaze coat ▶ 2tbsp. acrylic glazing liquid (transparent) / 1tbsp. monestial green artists' acrylic color / 1tbsp. titanium white artists' acrylic color
Sealant coat ▶ 1 pint (500ml.) matte acrylic varnish**

EQUIPMENT

**For trunk—metal rule / pencil / adjustable workbench and/or C-clamps / backsaw / medium-grade sandpaper / right-angled triangle / ruler or straightedge / protective mask (if using MDF) / jigsaw / drill with wood, 1in. (25mm.) flat wood and metal bits / screwdriver
For paint effect—mixing sticks / 1 x 2in. (50mm.) tossaway brush / container for mixing glaze / large plate / 1 x ½in. (12mm.) round hoghair brush / 1 x 2in. (50mm.) varnish brush**

Preparation

ALWAYS WEAR A MASK IF CUTTING MDF.

1 Measure the internal length and width of your trunk and make a note of those measurements—you will need to refer to them several times. Our trunk measured 20 x 29in. (50.5 x 73.5cm.).

2 To make the battens that support the board under the cushion, measure and mark two lengths and two widths on the 1 x 2in. (25 x 50mm.) wood, making both widths 2in. (5cm.) shorter than the internal measurement. This allows space for them to abut at the four corners. Our two widths were 18in. (45.5cm.) long.

3 Securing the wood with clamps, cut the four pieces as marked, using the backsaw. Sand carefully to remove any rough edges.

4 For the board, draw a rectangle on the wood, using the triangle and ruler (or straightedge). Make both length and width 1in. (2.5cm.) shorter than the internal measurements for easier removal. Ours was 19 x 28in. (48 x 71cm.). You could ask the lumberyard to precut to size if you prefer.

5 Clamp the wood, cut out the rectangle with the jigsaw, and sand any rough edges.

6 Use the flat wood bit to drill a hole approx. 3in. (7.5cm.) from each end of the board. You'll use these to lift it out of the trunk, so make them large enough to take at least one finger comfortably. Again, sand the rough edges.

Construction Ask someone to hold each of the battens in position as you drill holes for the screws which will secure them. The upper edge of the battens should be at the same height—approx. 1in. (2.5cm.) below the rim of the trunk, placed wide side down. Using the metal bit, drill from the outside to make three evenly spaced holes in the longer sides and two in the short sides. Insert the screws and tighten with the screwdriver.

Verdigris finish See page 167 for the technique. Again paint the inside of the lid and the entire outside. Stipple the surface details carefully.

Sealant coat Stir the varnish well, and apply two coats to your painted surfaces. Allow 2–3 hours for each coat to dry.

MAKING THE CUSHION

Use flame-retardant foam for the filling. For the Verdigris and Gingham trunks, I used a foam pad 4in. (10cm.) thick, cut ½in. (12mm.) wider and longer than the board. For the smaller French Trunk the pad was 3in. (7.5cm.) thick. Remember that it must fit inside the lid when closed.

Cut two rectangles of tartan to fit, adding ⅝in. (15mm.) all around for seams. I used approx. 2yd. (2m.) of 56in. (140cm.)-wide fabric for the two large trunks and 1yd. (1m.) for the small one. For the long sides, cut two pieces to fit, adding the same allowance to all edges. Repeat for the short sides.

Machine stitch the short ends of the sides together to make one long strip. Placing right sides together and matching seams to corners, machine stitch the long strip to one rectangle. Repeat to join the other rectangle, leaving one end open. Press the seams open, trimming and clipping the corners. Turn right side out, insert the pad, and slipstitch the open end.

COUNTRY FRENCH

CLEANING AND PRIMING I chose not to clean or prime this one so that the rust would break through quickly to enhance the aged effect.

MATERIALS Preparation and Construction—see Verdigris Trunk. This one was approx. half the size of the other two.
Base coat ▶ 8½ fl. oz. (250ml.) white latex flat paint
Top coat (outside) ▶ 8½ fl. oz. (250ml.) white latex flat paint
Top coat (inside) ▶ 6½ fl. oz. (190ml.) white latex flat paint / 4tbsp. dioxazine purple artists' acrylic color
Rust effect ▶ 3tbsp. reddish gold acrylic paint

THREE WAYS WITH A METAL TRUNK

EQUIPMENT

**For trunk—see Verdigris Trunk
For paint effect—mixing sticks / 2 x 2in. (50mm.) latex brushes /
container for mixing paint / hammer / chisel / saucer / 1 x 1in.
(25mm.) tossaway brush**

INSTRUCTIONS

For Preparation and Construction, see Verdigris Trunk.

Base coat

Stir the white latex paint well, and, using one of the latex brushes, apply a good, even coat to the prepared and primed inside lid and entire outside. Allow to dry (2–3 hours).

Top coats

1 Stirring well, brush another 8½ fl. oz. (250ml.) white latex paint onto the outside only; allow to dry (2–3 hours).
2 Pour 6½ fl. oz. (190ml.) white latex paint into the container, add the dioxazine purple, and stir well.
3 Apply to the inside lid, using the other latex brush. Allow to dry (2–3 hours).

Distressing the paint

Gently chip away at the edges and raised areas on the outside, using the hammer and chisel to reveal the bare metal beneath. Don't overdo it. Remember: the aim is to create natural aging and battering, not some lost-and-found reject.

Rust effect

Pouring a little of the reddish gold paint at a time into the saucer, dip just the tip of the small tossaway brush and apply the paint carefully to the chipped areas. Here again, your aim is to suggest just the first stages of rust, so don't cover the chips completely. Allow to dry (1 hour).

Making the cushion

See page 113. Contrasting piping would look great here.

THREE WAYS WITH A METAL TRUNK

BLUE GINGHAM

CLEANING AND PRIMING
Prepare the surface thoroughly by cleaning; prime inside of lid and outside with two coats of gray metal primer. See pages 12–17.

MATERIALS
Preparation and Construction—see Verdigris Trunk
Base coats ▸ 13½ fl. oz. (400ml.) white latex flat paint / 3½ fl. oz. (100ml.) cerulean blue artists' acrylic color (2 coats)
Rolling grid ▸ 1st stripe—5½ fl. oz (160ml.) white latex flat paint / 6 tbsp. ultramarine blue artists' acrylic color / 2nd stripe—4 fl. oz. (120ml.) white latex flat / 4 fl. oz. (120ml.) ultramarine blue
External detail ▸ 2 tbsp. premixed deep yellow latex flat paint
Sealant coat ▸ 1 pint (500ml.) clear matte acrylic varnish

EQUIPMENT
For trunk—see Verdigris Trunk
For paint effect—3 containers for mixing paint / mixing sticks / 1 x 2in. (50mm.) latex brush / china marker or soft colored pencil (to match stripes) / ruler or straightedge / right-angled triangle / 2 large plates / 2 x 1in. (25mm.) foam seam rollers / 1 x ½in. (12mm.) flat artists' brush / 1 x 2in. (50mm.) varnish brush

INSTRUCTIONS
For Preparation and Construction see Verdigris Trunk

Roller tartan
See page 162. I rolled a grid of medium and deep blue stripes over two coats of turquoise. The details were highlighted in yellow, using the artists' brush. Allow to dry (2 hours).

Sealant coat
See Verdigris Trunk.

Making the cushion
See page 113. Again, try piping—you can buy it readymade.

CRUSTACEAN

The shells you gathered on vacation needn't sit forlornly on a shelf. You can use them to create original objets d'art for bedrooms, living rooms, and bathrooms. Add some shells bought from specialist dealers—the variety is extraordinary. Bed them in tile adhesive applied with a filling knife—don't be too lavish or it will be difficult to paint— and leave to dry (12 hours). Apply primer and top coat with a gentle, tapping wrist action for even coverage. Brush a little talc onto the top coat while still wet if you want an aged look; when dry, highlight detail with gilt cream. (See pages 27 for adhesives, pages 40–3 for sealants.)

Left: Baroque splendor for a simple modern mirror. The new frame was cut from MDF (see template on page 183), glued to the old one, and secured with finishing nails. The main features—plaster cherubs, not shells—were bedded in first, followed by scraps of sheer curtain fabric, arranged in folds stiffened with diluted white glue. Coins, beads, and shells filled the empty spaces. Colorway: white acrylic primer; top coat—premixed mint green latex flat paint.

Left: This free-standing cornice, made with three pieces of 1 x 3in (25 x 75mm) wood, was glued and secured with finishing nails. It looked best cut narrower than the cabinet. The beauty of the scallops and their position dictated a formal approach, so small shells and beads fill the gaps. A silver-pointed textured wallpaper border decorates each door frame. Colorway: white acrylic primer; top coat—see page 52.

Left: Cooler color and just a little talc play down the divine decadence, but the texturing is still exuberant. The fabric shade is sponged (see page 170, Glaze coat), using 4 oz (120ml) acrylic glazing liquid, 1tbsp. white latex paint, 1tsp dioxazine purple artists' acrylic, and decorated with flat shells and little pieces of seaweed from a bathroom potpourri. Colorway: white acrylic primer; top coat—as shade.

DECORATED
HEADBOARD

It was a friend's complaint that she just could not find a well-designed, wooden headboard for her Hollywood bed that set me thinking here. The answer was blindingly simple—mount bedroom cabinet doors on a supporting panel, add small side shelves for a light or some books, and decorate. Note: this bed was only 54in. (1.37m.) wide. For a wider one, cut a larger panel on which to group or space your doors.

CLEANING AND PRIMING

Prepare the surface thoroughly before and after construction by cleaning; prime the front only. See pages 12–17.

MATERIALS

Preparation ▶ ½in. (12mm.) MDF or plywood (3ft x 3ft.[1m x 1m.])
Construction ▶ ⅜in. (9mm.) MDF or plywood, precut to size (19 x 61in.[48.3 x 155cm.]) / 4 bedroom cabinet doors (15 x 18in. [38 x 45.7cm.]) / 7 fl. oz. (210ml.) panel adhesive / 12 screws
Base coat ▶ 15½ fl. oz. (460ml.) white latex flat paint / 2tbsp. raw umber artists' acrylic color
Moldings ▶ 4 fl. oz. (120ml.) gold leaf paint / 5tbsp. cobalt blue artists' acrylic color
Decoration ▶ 2⅔tbsp. gold leaf paint / 3⅓tbsp. vermilion artists' acrylic color / 5tsp. emerald green artists' acrylic color
Aging ▶ 5 fl. oz. (150ml.) furniture wax (clear) / 2tbsp. burnt umber artists' oil color / 1tsp. Venetian red artists' oil color
Fixing the headboard ▶ 2 x 1 x 2in. (25 x 50mm.) battens, cut to size (see below) / approx. 20 screws

EQUIPMENT

Photocopier / metal rule / scissors / pencil / adjustable workbench and/or C-clamps / protective mask (if using MDF) / jigsaw / ruler or straightedge / right-angled triangle / 1 x 2in. (50mm.) tossaway brush / drill with wood bit / screwdriver / container for mixing paint / mixing sticks / 1 x 2in. (50mm.) latex brush / 2 small, flat artists' brushes / 3 artists' detail brushes / 5 saucers / stencil paper approx. 17 x 24in. (43 x 61cm.) / masking tape / cutting mat / X-Acto knife / lint-free cotton rags / 1 x ½in. (12mm.) stencil brush / medium-grade sandpaper / backsaw

INSTRUCTIONS
Preparation

ALWAYS WEAR A MASK IF CUTTING MDF.

1 Using a photocopier, enlarge the two shelf templates (for the base and backplate) on page 184 to size. The base sections of our shelves measured 6¼in. (16cm.) at their widest point, and our backplates were 5½in. (14cm.) high. Cut out.
2 Lay the templates for both sections on the ½in. (12mm.) wood, and, using the pencil, draw around the shapes. You need to cut two copies of each piece.
3 Clamp the wood to secure it, and cut out with the jigsaw.

DECORATED HEADBOARD

Construction

1 Use the ruler (or straightedge), triangle, and pencil to mark a line ½in. (12mm.) from the edge on all four sides of the precut sheet of wood. This defines the area where the doors are to be positioned—lay them down to check for fit.

2 Apply panel adhesive to the reverse of the doors with the tossaway brush, and place them side by side inside the pencil line. Allow to dry (12 hours).

3 You need two pairs of hands to assemble the shelves. Clamp one of the backplates upside down, and place a base section on top of it, at right angles and aligned with the tapering end of the backplate. Carefully drill two screw holes through the base and into the backplate and screw together. Repeat for the other shelf.

4 Clamp the headboard face down on your work surface so that at least 8in. (20cm.) overhangs the edge. Then clamp the shelves in their appropriate positions on either side, with the overlapping sections of the backplates uppermost. Drill eight screw holes though each backplate into the headboard, and screw together.

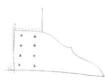

Base coat

1 Pour the latex paint into the container, add the raw umber, and stir well.

2 Apply an even coat to the prepared and primed surface with the latex brush. Allow to dry (2–3 hours).

Moldings

1 Stir the gold paint well, and, using one of the flat artists' brushes, paint the outer molding of each door frame and a narrow band around each front edge. Allow to dry (1 hour).

2 Using one of the detail brushes, paint the edges of the shelves with gold paint, and allow to dry (1 hour). Our doors had a slightly raised central section which partly echoed the shape of the inner molding of the door frame, so I also applied a narrow band of gold paint approx. ¼in. (5mm.) wide at the edge of each of them, too.

3 Place the cobalt blue in a saucer and stir well. Using the other flat brush, apply paint to the inner molding of each door frame. Allow to dry (1 hour).

Decoration

I used a mixture of stenciling (for the initials and bee motifs) and freehand painting (for the flowers). The stencils were placed first, using gold paint; see page 159, Stippling, for making and using stencils, and page 184 for the bee motif. Books and magazines offer an enormous variety of references for type styles—photocopy a few and experiment before making stencils for your chosen initials. (I'm not sure which came first—the initials or the bee—but both were clearly inspired by Napoleon and Josephine.) The flowers were added with two detail brushes, the vermilion before the green—both colors being placed on saucers and stirred well—and each color was allowed to dry (30 minutes).

Aging

1 Using medium-grade sandpaper, rub the surface in the direction of the grain to distress the decoration and reveal some of the base coat beneath. Wipe clean with damp rags.

2 See page 146, Aging with Wax, to age further (and seal) with a dark wax.

Attaching the headboard

Detail will vary according to the style of your bed base, but the basic approach will be the same. Two 1 x 2in. (25 x 50cm.) battens are cut with the backsaw and screwed to the back of the headboard and to the bed base or legs. Their length is determined by two things: the position of the lower fixing and the height you want the headboard to be.

FABRIC HANGINGS

Here's another advance in the crusade for imaginative hangings. This time the emphasis is on fabric and the focus is twin beds, although all three designs could be adapted for a double. Looking at the final results, I'm struck by how easy it is to create a different look with the same basic idea—something it would be fun to explore with the canopy—and how much a hangings can do to set the mood of a room.

MOORISH CANOPY

CLEANING AND PRIMING

Prepare the surface after construction by cleaning and priming the outside of the tester and fronts of the tiebacks. See pages 12–17.

MATERIALS

Preparation ▶ ⅜in. (9mm.) plywood or MDF (1yd x 1yd.[1m x 1m.]) / 1 x 2in. (25 x 50cm.) batten (½yd. [0.5m.] long) / 1½in. (38mm.) dowel (½yd. [0.5m.] long)
Construction ▶ 5 fl. oz. (150ml.) wood glue / 10 finishing nails / 5 fl. oz. (150ml.) fine-grade, ready-mixed wood filler / 2 glass drapery finials
Base coat ▶ 3½ fl. oz. (100ml.) silver spray paint
Glaze coat ▶ 5 fl. oz. (150ml.) acrylic glazing liquid (transparent) / 2tbsp. Payne's gray artists' acrylic color / 2tsp. Mars black artists' acrylic color
Sealant coat ▶ 8½ fl. oz. (250ml.) clear matte acrylic varnish
Fitting the draperies ▶ cotton muslin (7½yd. x 48in. [7m. x 120cm.]) / 1 spool matching thread / 8½ fl. oz. (250ml.) silver fabric paint
Mounting the canopy ▶ 6 screws and anchors (see pages 27–8) / 18in. (0.5m.) steel wire / 30–40 metal beads / 6 small screw eyes

EQUIPMENT

Photocopier / scissors / pencil / adjustable workbench and/or C-clamps / protective mask / jigsaw / medium-grade sandpaper / metal rule / drill with wood and masonry bits / backsaw / 1 x ½in. (12mm.) round fitch / tack hammer / filling knife / screwdriver / masking tape (optional) / plastic drop cloth / container for mixing glaze / mixing stick / large plate / 1 x ½in. (12mm.) round hoghair brush / 1 x 1in. (25mm.) varnish brush / iron / needle / sewing machine (optional) / clean drop cloth / small, round artists' brush / hand-held staple gun and appropriate staples / spirit level / ruler or straightedge / tinsnips / pliers

INSTRUCTIONS
Preparation

ALWAYS WEAR A MASK IF CUTTING MDF OR SPRAYING. PROTECT YOUR WORK SPACE WITH DROP CLOTHS AND WORK IN A WELL-VENTILATED AREA.

1 Using a photocopier, enlarge the templates for the tester and the tiebacks on page 184 to the appropriate size. The front section of our tester was 13¾in. (35cm.) wide. You can make the tester bigger, of course, but you are likely to run into assembly problems if you make it smaller.

2 Cut out the full-sized templates, lay them on the wood, and use a pencil line to make one copy of the front section, two of the side section, and two of the tieback backplate.

3 Secure the wood with C-clamps, and carefully cut out all five shapes, using the jigsaw. Rub with sandpaper to smooth any rough edges.

4 Measeure, mark, and then drill a central screw hole in each tieback backplate.

5 Using the backsaw, trim the batten to the width of the front section of the tester minus ¾in. (18mm.), which is the joint thickness of the two side sections. Drill a screw hole 2in. (5cm.) from each end of the batten through its 1in. (25mm.) measurement.

6 Cut two 5in. (12.5cm.) pieces of dowel, using the backsaw. Drill a small pilot hole at each end of both.

Construction

1 To assemble the tester, use the fitch to brush a thin strip of wood glue onto the back of each side of the front section, and position the side pieces at right angles to it. Working from the front of the tester and using the tack hammer, tap four finishing nails into each side to secure. Allow to dry (1 hour).

2 Glue the batten to the back of the tester at the base to form the fourth side of the rectangle, with a finishing nail tapped in through both sides.

3 Plug any holes with wood filler (applied with the filling knife), allow to dry (30 minutes), and sand down.

4 To assemble the tiebacks, attach the dowels to the backplates, screwing through the central holes from the back of the backplates, and then screw the finials into the free ends of the dowels. If you're worried about getting paint on the glass, mask the finials or attach them when mounting the canopy.

Pewter finish   See page 166 for the technique.

Sealant coat   Brush on an even coat of varnish, and allow to dry (4 hours).

Hanging the draperies

1 Press carefully with an iron, then cut the fabric in half to make two panels—ours were both 11½ft. (3.5m.) long. Hem the sides and bottom of each one, using a machine for speed.

2 Protect your working surface with the drop cloth, stir the silver paint well, and use the artists' brush to paint random swirls and dots on both panels. Allow to dry (20 minutes).

3 To seal the paint, turn the fabric over and press the reverse with a medium iron.

4 Using the needle and thread, gather the unhemmed top of one drapery to fit half the tester. Check for fit—you are aiming for even pleating—and then staple in place, again working from the front. Repeat for the other drapery panel

Mounting the canopy

1 Another pair of hands is essential for this stage. Decide on the height of the tester. Draw two faint pencil lines on the wall to mark the position of the batten at the back, and check that they are straight, using the spirit level. Mark the positions of the two screw holes—they must correspond exactly to the holes you drilled in the batten.

2 Using the masonry bit, drill the holes and secure the tester as appropriate (see pages 27–8).

3 Drape one panel as shown to help you decide on the height and position of the tiebacks. Mark and then check the placing of each backplate on the wall with the spirit level and a ruler (or straightedge) with the masonry bit, drill through the top and bottom of each backplate into the wall.

4 Secure as appropriate (see pages 26–7) and drape the fabric.

5 Cut the wire into three pieces, using the tinsnips, and twist a retaining loop at one end of each piece with the pliers. Thread the beads and hang each length on a screw eye screwed into the lower edge of the tester, making pilot holes with the bradawl.

FABRIC HANGINGS

SHAKER HANGING

CLEANING AND PRIMING

Clean the surface thoroughly after preparation (see below) and by priming just the front of the peg rail. See pages 12–17.

MATERIALS

Preparation ▶ Shaker or similar peg rail
Base and top coats ▶ 3½ fl. oz. (100ml.) white latex semigloss paint / 10 fl. oz. (300ml.) red-violet artists' acrylic color / 3⅓ tbsp. deep violet artists' acrylic color / 3⅓ tbsp. permanent violet artists' acrylic color
Sealant coat ▶ 5 fl. oz. (150ml.) furniture wax (clear)
Preparing the hanging ▶ 8¼ ft. x 56in. [2.5m. x 140cm.]) natural, unbleached, drapery-weight linen / 1 spool matching thread
Stamping ▶ 1 x 3½ fl. oz. (100ml.) brown fabric ink pad
Fixing the peg rail ▶ screws and anchors (see pages 27–8)

EQUIPMENT

Container for mixing paint / mixing stick / 1 x 1in. (25mm.) latex brush / lint-free cotton rags / metal rule / scissors / iron / sewing machine / 1in. (25mm.)-wide ruler / needle / pins / assorted rubber stamps / spirit level / straightedge / drill with masonry bit, plus, if required (see Preparation), adjustable workbench and/or C-clamps / backsaw / wood bit / medium-grade sandpaper

INSTRUCTIONS
Preparation

If you need to shorten your peg rail, secure it with clamps, measure, and cut to size, using the backsaw. Ours was 62in. (157cm.) long. Sand any rough edges, and remember to drill a new screw hole at the cut end.

Base and top coats

Pour the white latex paint into the container, add all three violets stir well. Apply two coats to the prepared and primed surfaces, 2–3 hours for each to dry.

Sealant coat

Using a clean rag and a circular movement, apply the wax to the painted surfaces; allow to set (15 minutes). Buff up with a clean rag.

Preparing the hanging

1 For the hanging, measure and cut one piece of fabric 46in. (1.17m.) deep x 81in. (2.06m.) wide. From the remaining fabric, cut 14 ties, each 14 x 4in. (35.5 x 10cm.).
2 To hem the hanging, turn under 1in. (2.5cm.) at the sides and bottom and 2in. (5cm.) at the top, press with an iron, and machine stitch.
3 Fold the ties in half lengthwise (right sides together) and press. Stitch one end and long side of each, taking seams of approx. ½in. (12mm.).

4 To turn the ties inside out, place the short, stitched end of one tie over one end of the ruler, and roll the fabric down over it, until the tie is right side out. Press, tuck in unstitched ends; slipstitch.

5 Working on the wrong side of the hanging, pin pairs of ties side by side along the top hem. Space the pairs evenly 9½in. (24cm.) apart, leaving approx. 4in. (10cm.) at each end. Stitch in place.

Stamping the motifs

See page 165, Using Ink stamp Pads. I used readymade leaf and feather designs.

Fixing the peg rail

Decide on the position of the rail, mark, and check with a spirit level and straightedge. Drill the holes in the wall, using the masonry bit, and secure as appropriate (see pages 27–8).

FABRIC HANGINGS

CLEANING	Prepare the surface thoroughly. See pages 12–17. Do not prime.

MATERIALS — **Staining the pole ▶ 5 fl. oz. (150ml.) acrylic varnishing wax (clear) / 3⅓ tbsp. emerald green artists' acrylic color / 1½in. (38mm.) dowel, precut to size, 62in. (157cm.) long**
Preparing the banner ▶ 5ft. x 51in. (1.5m. x 130cm.) duck canvas / 1 spool matching thread
Stenciling the flags ▶ 7 fl. oz. (200ml.) fabric paint in white, yellow, ultramarine, and bright red / black fabric pen
Fixing the banner ▶ 2 large ring screw-in drapery finials / 2 brass brackets to fit dowel, plus screws and anchors (see pages 27–8)

EQUIPMENT — **Container for mixing stain / mixing stick / 1 x 1in. (25mm.) tossaway brush / metal rule / scissors / iron / sewing machine / right-angled triangle / ruler or straightedge / pencil / photocopier / 2 x stencil papers approx. 17 x 24in. (43 x 61cm.) / masking tape / X-Acto knife / cutting mat / lint-free cotton rags / 4 saucers / 4 x 1in. (25mm.) stencil brushes / pins / spirit level / drill with masonry bit**

INSTRUCTIONS
Staining the pole

1 Pour the wax into the container, add the emerald green acrylic paint, and stir well.
2 Using the tossaway brush, apply the stain to the prepared surface in the direction of the grain. Take care not to overload the brush. Allow to dry (2–3 hours).

Preparing the banner

1 Measure and cut one piece of canvas 54in. (137cm.) deep x 59in. (150cm.) wide and four flag pockets, each 8½in. (22cm.) deep x 12¾in. (32cm.) wide.
2 Turn under 1in. (2.5cm.) at the sides of the banner and 2in. (5cm.) at bottom to make a hem. Turn under 4in. (10cm.) at the top to create a casing or open-ended hem for the pole. Press with a hot iron, and machine stitch.
3 Turn 1in. (2.5cm.) under on all four sides of the pockets and press, again with a hot iron.

4 Use the metal rule, ruler (or straightedge), triangle, and pencil to mark the positions of all the flags on the front of the banner (the side without hems). The photograph on page 185 gives a complete view of it: the top row is approx. 4in. (10cm.) from the upper edge, the bottom row 6½in. (16.5cm.) from the lower edge, and there is a 2in. (5cm.) margin at both sides.

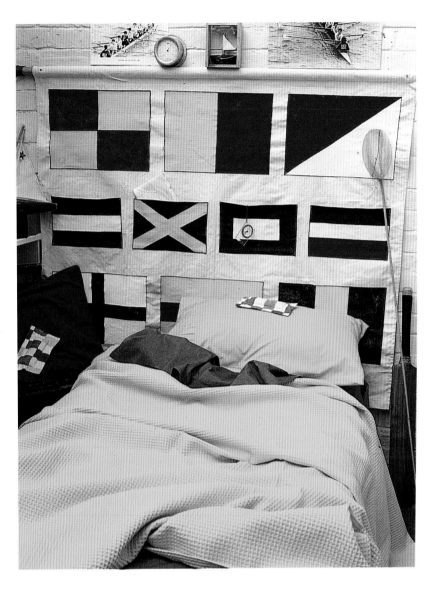

Stenciling the flags See page 159, Stippling, for making and using stencils, and page 185 for the motifs, and color guide. I used ready-mixed fabric paints and drew lines around the completed flags with a fabric pen and ruler to neaten them. Iron the reverse of the canvas carefully on a medium setting to seal the paint.

Finishing the banner **1** Pin the pockets in place as marked to form the center row, keeping the pins away from the edges.
2 Machine stitch approx. ¼in. (5mm.) from the edge around the sides and bottom of each one.
3 Push the pole through the casing at the top. Screw in the finials.

Fixing the banner Decide on the bracket positions, mark, and check with a spirit level and straightedge. Drill the holes in the wall, using a masonry bit, and secure as appropriate (see pages 27–8).

DOUBLE BED
TO FOUR-POSTER

The principle behind the transformation of this simple pine bed frame is extremely versatile. Change the fabric for something pale and floaty, with a paint finish to match, and you've got a romantic look.

CLEANING AND PRIMING

Prepare the surface by cleaning before and after construction and by priming. See pages 12–17.

MATERIALS

Preparation ▶ 1¼in. (31mm.) dowel—4 x 76in. (193cm.) for posts; 1in. (25mm.) dowel—2 x 51in. (129.5cm.) for end poles, ¾in. (19mm.) dowel—2 x 78in. (198cm.) for side poles, precut by lumberyard

Base coat (posts) ▶ 9fl. oz. (270ml.) white latex flat paint / 2tbsp. raw umber artists' acrylic color

First stripe ▶ 5½fl. oz. (160ml.) white latex flat paint / 4tbsp. dioxazine purple artists' acrylic color / 2tbsp. cadmium red artists' acrylic color

Second stripe ▶ 5½fl. oz. (160ml.) white latex flat paint / 6tbsp. yellow ocher artists' acrylic color

Aging posts ▶ 3½fl. oz. (100ml.) furniture wax (clear) / 5tsp. burnt umber artists' oil color / 5tsp. yellow ocher artists' oil color

Base coat (finials) ▶ screw-in wood finials / 5⅓tbsp. white latex flat paint / 2tsp. burnt umber artists' acrylic color

Size coat ▶ 3½fl. oz. (100ml.) water-based size

Gilding ▶ 10–12 loose sheets imitation gold leaf

Distressing ▶ 5tbsp. denatured alcohol

Sealant (finials) ▶ 3½fl. oz. (100ml.) transparent polish

Aging finials ▶ 1tbsp. cadmium red artists' acrylic color / ½tbsp. medium gray artists' acrylic color / ½tbsp. white latex flat paint / 1½tbsp. water

Woodwash (base and poles) ▶ 3½fl. oz. (100ml.) white latex flat paint / 3⅓tbsp. cadmium red artists' acrylic color / 3⅓tbsp. medium gray artists' acrylic color / 5 fl. oz. (150ml.) water

Construction ▶ 20 screws, as required (see below) / ½fl. oz. (15ml.) fine, ready-mixed wood filler

Hangings ▶ 19ft. x 56in. (6m. x 140cm.) Venetian red cotton / 10ft. x 56in. (3m. x 140cm.) ocher cotton / matching thread / 6 shells / 5 fl. oz. (150ml.) gold acrylic spray paint

DOUBLE BED TO FOUR-POSTER

EQUIPMENT

Metal rule / pencil / adjustable workbench and/or C-clamps / drill with wood and 1in. (25mm.) flat wood bits / 1in. (25mm.) masking tape (two rolls) / chisel or heavy-duty utility knife / 6 containers for mixing paint, glaze, and wash / mixing sticks / 2 x 2in. (50mm.) latex brushes / 3 x 1in. (25mm.) latex brushes / flat artists' brush / medium-grade sandpaper / lint-free cotton rags / water to dampen rags / saucer / 1 x 1in. (25mm.) flat bristle brush / disposable gloves / 1 x 1in. (25mm.) round, soft-bristled brush / clean dustcloths / fine-grade steel wool / screwdriver / stepladder / filling knife / tailors' chalk / scissors / pins / sewing machine / needle / iron / hand-held staple gun and staples

INSTRUCTIONS

Preparation

1 To mark the holes into which the end poles will fit, use the metal rule and pencil to make a cross 1in. (2.5cm.) from one end of each post.

2 Secure each post in turn with clamps, and carefully drill a hole ½in. (12mm.) deep, using the 1in. (25mm.) flat wood bit and marking the depth on the drill bit with tape (see page 29).

3 To mark the holes into which the side poles will fit, lay all four posts on a flat surface with the tops side by side and the drill holes all facing upward. Turn each one to the right 90 degrees, and mark a cross at right angles to the first hole approx. 3in. (7.5cm.) from the same end.

4 Clamping as before, carefully drill all four holes approx. ½in. (12mm.) deep.

5 To improve the fit of the posts when screwed to the bed, you need to flattten a strip approx. 1in. (2.5cm.) wide at the bottom of each one. The lengths will be determined by the height of your bed base—our strips were 15in. (38cm.) long. Position your posts to measure the required length(s), making sure each strip aligns with the upper hole at the other end.

6 Clamping each post in turn, use the chisel (or heavy-duty utility knife) to make the required strips.

7 Position each post against the appropriate bed leg, and drill three evenly spaced pilot holes for the screws that will secure it once painting is completed.

Base coat (posts)

1 Pour the white latex paint into one of the containers, add the raw umber, and stir well.

2 Using one of the large latex brushes, apply an even coat to the prepared and primed surfaces. Allow to dry (2–3 hours). Reserve any remaining color here and after the next two stages for final retouching (see Construction, step 7).

Adding the stripes (posts)

1 Starting at the base, carefully wind the masking tape around each post in spirals 2in. (5cm.) apart.

2 Pour the white latex paint into a second container, add the dioxazine purple and cadmium red, and stir well. Apply to the unmasked stripe on each post with a small latex brush. Allow to dry (2–3 hours), then gently remove the tape.

3 Mix the white latex paint and yellow ocher and use the artists' brush to paint an ocher stripe on the cream, leaving a narrow cream stripe on either side. Allow to dry (2–3 hours).

DOUBLE BED TO FOUR-POSTER

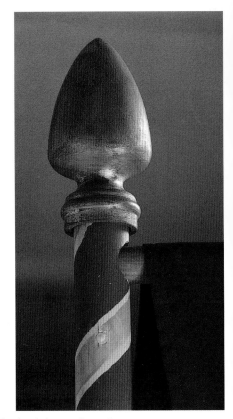

Aging the posts

1 Using medium-grade sandpaper, rub the posts lightly to reveal some of the base coat, and wipe clean with damp rag.

2 To seal and darken, see page 146, Aging with Wax, step 1. Apply the wax with a clean rag, following the direction of the stripes. Leave to set (approx. 15 minutes), and buff with another clean rag.

Gilding (finials)

See page 168 for the technique. I mixed a terracotta base coat to create a mellow effect and, before sealing, distressed the gilding by rubbing very gently to reveal some of the base color. Use fine-grade steel wool and denatured alcohol, dabbed on with a clean cotton rag.

Aging the finials

1 Place the white latex paint in a container. Add the cadmium red, medium gray, and water (a little at a time), stirring well to mix.

2 Apply, using one of the small latex brushes.

3 Work quickly over the surface with clean rags folded into a pad, removing any excess glaze but leaving some in areas of detail. Allow to dry (1 hour).

Woodwashing (base and poles)

See page 140 for the technique. I used a single wash coat mixed to create a harmonizing Venetian red.

Construction

Ask someone to help you throughout this stage.

1 Position and secure each post, using the screw holes drilled before painting.

2 Working at one end of the bed, fit one of the end poles into the two upper holes in the posts.

3 To hold the pole in position, drill a hole through each post and into the pole. Screw to secure. Believe me—a stepladder is essential. For safety's sake and for accuracy, you must be at the correct height.

4 Repeat steps 2 and 3 to erect the pole at the other end.

5 Using the same method, erect both side poles, fitting them into the two lower holes in the posts.

6 Screw in the finials.

7 Conceal the screws with wood filler, leave to dry (1 hour), and sand gently. Paint with the appropriate colors.

Hangings

1 Lay the red cotton on a flat surface and, using tailors' chalk and the metal rule, mark and cut four long pieces. Our bed was approx. 74 x 54in. (188 x 137cm.), and I made the pieces each 9¾ft. x 16½in. (3m. x 42cm.), adding ⅝in. (15mm.) seam allowance all around. You will need to adjust these measurements if your bed is longer or shorter, wider or narrower. If you do, remember to allow enough fabric for an elegant drape over the bed.

2 Using the same method, cut two pieces of the same size from the ocher cotton.

3 Lay one of the pieces on a flat surface, fold neatly in half lengthwise, measure 8in. (20.5cm.) from one end along the cut edges, and mark with chalk or a pin. Carefully turn back the upper half of the folded fabric from this mark to make a diagonal fold. Pinning first if you prefer, cut along the fold, and then, using your first cut as a guide, cut across the lower half. Repeat for the point at the other end. Now shortcut the process by using this piece as a pattern to cut a point at each end of all the other pieces.

4 Pair two red pieces to make one panel, placing them right sides together. Pin along the edges and machine stitch, leaving one side of one point open. Repeat, pairing the other two red pieces, then the two ocher pieces.

5 Turn right side out, tuck in the raw edges, slipstitch neatly with needle and thread and press each panel with a hot iron.

6 Use the machine to topstitch all around each panel approx. ¼in. (5mm.) from the edge.

7 Sew found objects to the tip of each point with needle and thread. I chose shells, drilled a hole in each one, then sprayed them gold and allowed them to dry (15 minutes).

8 Using the stepladder, drape the panels over both end poles and secure with the staple gun.

PART THREE

TECHNIQUES

A versatile range of paint finishes for furniture in traditional and contemporary colorways, plus decorative effects using ceramic, fabric, rush, glass, and metal, all explained with step-by-step instructions

A witty treatment for a mosaic table top: this effect was achieved with a mix of tiles and crockery. The tiles used for the blue background were probably broken randomly (see the basic technique on pages 174–6) but the "plate" was certainly cut with tile nippers from several plates of varying size and carefully assembled.

ABOUT TECHNIQUES

This section of the book, also, can be used in two ways. On one level, it's a straightforward resource for the major projects and ideas spreads in Part Two. In that context it provides detailed instructions on how to achieve the various paint finishes and decorative effects cited there, frequently suggesting alternative colorways and illustrating additional small makeover projects, from shelves to deckchairs, from stools to firescreens. On a second level, this section can, like Part Two, be the starting point for your own, totally original makeovers, providing endless scope for experimentation in a great range of different styles.

The paint finishes I've chosen to include are a hardworking bunch. Easy to apply and (with the notable exception of the daunting, but very simple, lacquer) quick to do, they will all serve you well. Some, such as gilding, dragging, crackle glaze, and colorwashing, have a long history; dragging, for example, was developed in the eighteenth century and used in the drawing rooms of the aspiring middle classes, who wanted the luxurious effect of fashionable silk-lined walls without the expense. Others, like woodwashing, have almost no past—I reckon it must have sprung from some universal need to redress the balance as the taste for pine-stripping reached saturation point in the mid-eighties. But labels like "traditional" and "contemporary" are frequently meaningless where paint finishes are concerned.

An exercise in découpage using aged music scores (see page 160) has created a subject that suits this classical room admirably. It's possible that the chest has less grand origins— the turned legs could have been added for gravitas. Note that the front itself is painted to highlight the basic structure.

Take dragging, on page 150. My basic recipe for burnt umber on deep red does emulate the historical finish, using a darker on dark glaze, and works well on makeovers in period settings, whereas the light over dark effect in swatch 2 or the strong, "modern" oranges of swatch 4 create a much more fashionable look.

Color may be the defining element in any makeover scheme, but the technique is clearly important, too. Take a good hard look at your "raw material." Can you achieve the look you want with it? If the wood is not thick enough or the basic shape not suitable, change the game plan. Aged paint is never going to be a totally convincing disguise for the sleek lines of a wall of matte black laminate shelving.

But that said, some of my most successful makeovers have happened when I've ignored the cautious promptings of "taste." The metal effects on wood and laminate on pages 92–3 are a great example. Mix and match with some of the other decorative techniques I've included, using metal, glass, ceramic, and fabric, and you have a wonderfully potent brew. Why not team punched tin with water-based crackle glaze or set découpage on gilding?

Gain confidence and it's fun to experiment with mixing your own colors, too. Using the basic recipes and the advice on pages 32–3 as your guide, it's a satisfying exercise to create a unique tone which exactly captures, say, the color of a favorite fabric or a hand-painted tile picked up years ago on a foreign trip.

Finally, some practical points to remember. If designing your own makeovers, check the Preparation section on pages 12–17 and take account of the advice concerning sealants on pages 42–3. It's wise to practice your paint techniques on sample sheets primed with white paint first; masonite or heavy cardboard is adequate, though tests for woodwashing are best run on the appropriate wood.

Left: This stocky cabinet is exactly the kind of piece likely to languish in a junk shop for ages waiting for someone to love it. There's no special technique to call attention to here. It's just a good example of the way you can make old furniture work for you. Gloss paints have been chosen for their tough, bright good looks, but in a child's room I would opt for water-based paints, sealed with silk acrylic varnish.

Below: The wax-resist aged paint technique (see page 144) works best when used on sympathetic shapes. Try sienna tones for this colorway.

WOODWASHING

The name says it all—this simple technique creates a pale wash of color on wood, leaving grain and any other surface detail still apparent. It's an almost instant upgrade for cheap, unpainted softwoods, new or old, although there may be some surface preparation before you begin (see pages 12–17). If you're prepared to strip, you can woodwash painted pieces too, but I don't recommend committing to the idea before you see what the wood is like. Only a limited range of commercial washes is available, so making your own offers exciting scope for color experiment. Single washes are fine, but I illustrate the effects you can achieve with two—light on dark or dark on light.

BASIC RECIPE—ANTIQUE WHITE ON MOSS GREEN

MATERIALS

Quantities for Flexible Storage for Home Workers (see page 66)
**First wash coat ▶ 7 fl. oz. (210ml.) white latex flat paint /
4tbsp. emerald green artists' acrylic color / 1tbsp. cadmium yellow artists' acrylic color / 1tbsp. pale olive green artists' acrylic color / 6 fl. oz. (180ml.) water**
**Second wash coat ▶ 9 fl. oz. (270ml.) white latex flat paint /
2tbsp. raw umber artists' acrylic color / 6 fl. oz. (180ml.) water**

EQUIPMENT

2 containers for mixing washes / mixing sticks / 2 x 2in. (50mm.) latex brushes / lint-free cotton rags

INSTRUCTIONS
First wash coat

1 Pour the latex paint into one of the containers, add the acrylic color, and stir well.
2 Add the water (a little at a time) and stir again. You are aiming for the consistency of light cream.
3 Brush the thin wash onto the prepared but unpainted surface (see pages 12–17). Work, wherever possible, in the direction of the grain, which you will be able to see through the thin wash.
4 Using pads of clean rag, quickly wipe the surface to reveal more of the grain beneath. Allow to dry (1–2 hours).

Second wash coat

Mix and apply the second wash in the same way, using the other container and the second latex brush.

Notes If planning your own project, protect with a sealant for a hardwearing finish (see pages 42–3).

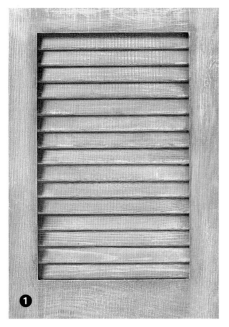

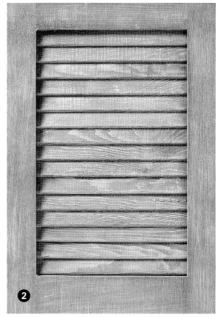

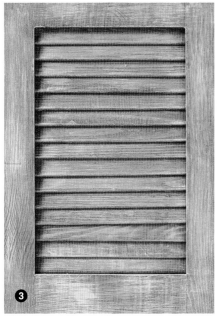

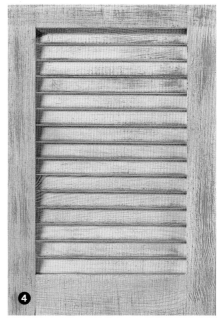

❶ ANTIQUE WHITE ON MOSS GREEN
The basic recipe: the use of a soft, creamy white over color creates an appealing, almost sun-kissed look.

❷ RASPBERRY ON DAMSON
1st wash: 5 oz (150ml) white latex flat; acrylics—3½ oz (100ml) dioxazine purple, 3⅓ tbsp cadmium red. 2nd: 7 oz (210ml) white latex flat; acrylic—3½ oz (100ml) rose pink.

❸ ANTIQUE WHITE ON RASPBERRY
1st wash: 7 oz (210ml) white latex flat; acrylics— 3tbsp cadmium red, 1tbsp raw umber. 2nd wash: 9 oz (270ml) white latex flat; artists' acrylic —2tbsp raw umber.

❹ MOSS GREEN ON YELLOW OCHER
1st wash: 8½ oz (250ml) white latex flat; acrylics — 2tbsps cadmium yellow and bright green. 2nd wash: 7 oz (210ml) white latex flat; acrylics— 4tbsp emerald green, 1tbsp each cadmium yellow and pale olive green.

HIGH-GLOSS LACQUER

Of course this is a cheat. The high-gloss finish of oriental lacquer, traditionally seen in black or red, was hard won by craftsmen prepared to lay down a thousand coats of resin—in later centuries paint—laboriously sanding each one back before the next was applied. Much as I love painting, I'm delighted that modern technologists, with their tough, oil-based gloss paints, can take most of the slog out of achieving this infinitely sleek, sophisticated look. Remember, I said "most." This essentially simple technique still takes care and time, but it is well worth persevering when the results are so stunning.

You need three other ingredients for success. The first is a good surface—no amount of subtle filling and patching will ever produce the mirror-like sheen that convinces. The second is a sound oil-based primer, which is why it's included here. The third is a dust-free place to paint. Good luck!

BASIC RECIPE—BRIGHT YELLOW

MATERIALS

Quantities for Contemporary Set of Drawers (see page 56)
Primer coat ▶ 1 pint (500ml.) white oil-based primer
Lacquer coats ▶ 1½ quarts (1.5 liters) premixed bright yellow high-gloss paint (5 coats)

EQUIPMENT

Mixing sticks / 2 x 2in. (50mm.) tossaway brushes / waterproof sandpaper / lint-free cotton rags / warm, soapy water

INSTRUCTIONS
Primer coat

1 Stir the oil-based primer well, and, using one of the tossaway brushes, apply a good, even coat to the prepared surface (see pages 12–13, 16–17). Allow to dry (4–6 hours).
2 Rub the surface smooth with waterproof sandpaper.
3 Using clean rags and warm, soapy water, wipe thoroughly to remove all the dust. Allow to dry completely.

Above left: The tough surface of a high-gloss finish is ideal for bathrooms, where condensation and changes of temperature can, in time, threaten some subtler effects.

Lacquer coats

1 Stir the gloss paint well. Apply an even coat to the surface with the other tossaway brush, working in the direction of the grain wherever appropriate. Try not to drag the paint too much, and yet avoid making short, fussy brush strokes. Allow to dry (12 hours if possible—8 hours at least).
2 Rub down the surface with waterproof sandpaper, remove any dust with a damp rag, and leave to dry.
3 Repeat steps 1 and 2 three times.
4 Repeat step 1 once more and leave to dry (12 hours).

❶ BRIGHT YELLOW
The lively color used for the basic recipe has an essentially modern feel and works well in dark, sunless rooms. But swatch test it first—you may need to adjust your lighting.

❷ NEARLY BLACK
For industrial-chic interiors, this dark gray with a hint of indigo will team successfully with chrome and steel.

❸ BRIGHT RED
A lighter shade of a traditional color, red lacquer will sit alongside dark antique woods or austere minimalism.

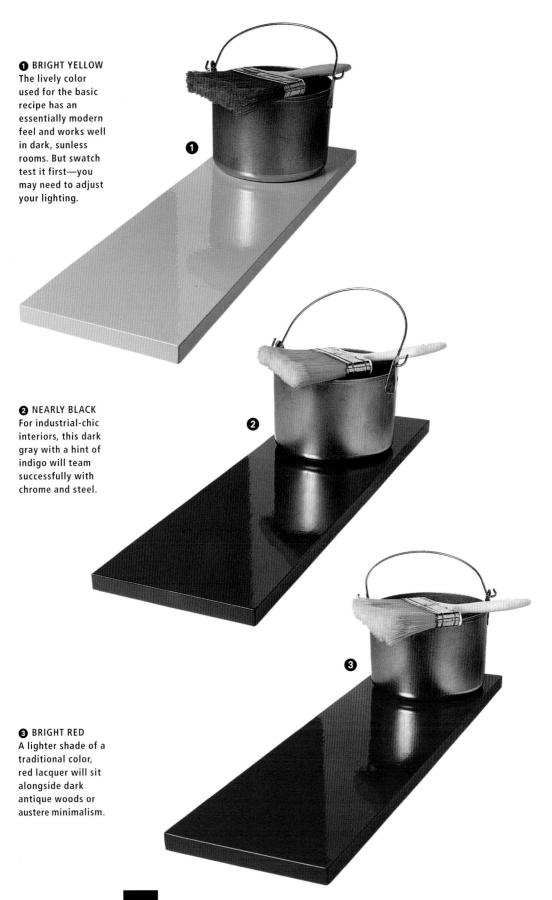

AGED PAINT

This group of techniques provides an invaluable aid for anyone keen to add a sense of history or character to undistinguished surfaces. All three are designed to simulate the effects of age on paintwork, either by distressing a painted surface to reveal an older, contrasting color beneath or by mellowing or dulling down an original color. You can, if you wish, take the process still further by literally attacking your surfaces with hammer and bradawl.

BASIC RECIPE—WAX-RESIST METHOD

MATERIALS	**Quantities for Bleached Wardrobe (see page 50)** **Base coat ▶ 1 pint (500ml.) white latex flat paint** **Wax resist ▶ 5 fl. oz. (150ml.) furniture wax** **Top coats ▶ 12½ fl. oz. (370ml.) white latex flat paint / 10 fl. oz. (300ml.) turquoise artists' acrylic color / 3½ fl. oz. (100ml.) monestial green artists' acrylic color (2 coats)**
EQUIPMENT	**Mixing sticks / 2 x 2in. (50mm.) latex brushes / 1 x 1in. (25mm.) round fitch / container to mix paint / fine-grade sandpaper / lint-free cotton rags**
INSTRUCTIONS **Base coat**	Stir well and apply to the prepared and primed surface (see pages 12–17) with one of the latex brushes. Allow to dry (2–3 hours).
Wax resist	Using the fitch, dab the wax lightly and evenly onto the areas where natural wear occurs—on knobs or handles, around the leading edge of doors, and on raised paneling or details. These are the places where the base coat will be revealed when the top coat is rubbed back. The more wax you apply, the more worn will be the effect. Allow to set (15 minutes).
Top coats	**1** Pour the latex paint into the container, add the color, and stir well. **2** Apply two coats to the surface, using the other latex brush. Allow 2–3 hours for each coat to dry.
Distressing the paint	**1** Using sandpaper, rub back to the base paint at the areas where you applied wax. Be prepared to take time over this stage—you'll have to rub quite heavily. **2** Smooth any rough paint edges with a final sanding, and wipe clean, using damp rags. **Notes** If planning your own project, protect with a sealant for a hardwearing finish (see pages 42–3).

❶ AQUA ON WHITE
The basic recipe and most heavily distressed of the examples; note how sections of the frame and panel have been worked to suggest years of exposure to sun and sea spray.

❷ DEEP BLUE ON DEEP YELLOW
I used a little less wax and sanding for a colorway that reminds me of the Mediterranean. Both colors are premixed.

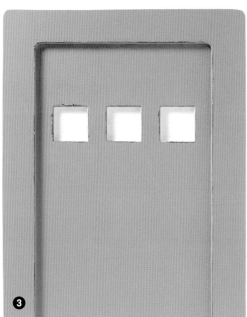

❸ LIME GREEN ON TERRACOTTA
Base coat: 10 oz (300ml) white latex flat; acrylics —5 oz (150ml) raw umber, 4tbsp chromium red. Top coat: 22 oz (650ml) white latex flat; acrylics—4tbsp emerald green, 1tbsp each cadmium yellow and pale olive green.

❹ LAVENDER ON WHITE
Treatment here and in example 3 is more refined. The result is a subtler effect, and one to try in rooms where you spend more time. Top coat: 24 oz (710ml) white latex flat; acrylic— 4tbsp dioxazine purple.

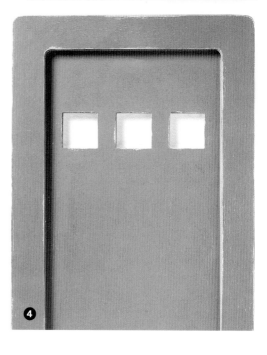

AGED PAINT

BASIC RECIPE—AGING WITH WAX

MATERIALS
Quantities for Fire screens (see below)
Wax coat ▶ 2tbsp. furniture wax (clear) / 1tbsp. yellow ocher artists' oil color

EQUIPMENT
Saucer / mixing stick / lint-free cotton rags

INSTRUCTIONS
Wax coat

1 Place the furniture wax on the saucer, add the oil color, and stir thoroughly.
2 Folding clean rags to make a pad, rub the wax evenly over the painted surface. Allow to set (15 minutes), and then buff up with another clean rag.

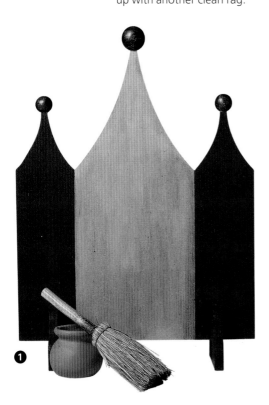

❶ WARM TONES Some colors seem to warm as they age, and the way the creamy white base coat of the center panel has taken the tone of the wax mixed for the basic recipe is a good example.

Base coats: (outer panels) 3½tbsp white latex flat, acrylics—2tbsp dioxazine purple, 4tsp cadmium red; (center panel) 4tsp white latex flat, acrylic—2tbsp yellow ocher.

❷ DARK TONES Most colors simply "dirty" or darken naturally over time. This wax is tinted with a mix of ½tbsp Payne's gray and ½tbsp Mars black oil color. Base coats:

(outer panels) 2⅔tbsp white latex flat, acrylics—2⅔tbsp monestial blue, 4tsp Payne's gray; (center panel) 2⅔tbsp white latex flat, acrylic—2tsp raw umber.

BASIC RECIPE—AGING WITH GLAZE

MATERIALS

Quantities for Shutters (see below)
Aging glaze ▶ 5tbsp. acrylic glazing liquid (transparent) /
1tbsp. monestial green artists' acrylic color / 2tsp. Payne's gray
artists' acrylic color

EQUIPMENT

**Container for mixing glaze / mixing stick / 1 x 1–2in. (25–50mm.)
latex brush**

INSTRUCTIONS

Aging glaze

1 Pour the glazing liquid into the container, add the color,
and stir well.
2 Dip just the tip of the dry brush into the glaze, and remove
any excess on the lip of the container, then apply glaze
evenly to the entire painted surface. Work in the same
direction(s) as the previous coat of paint, glaze, or varnish.
3 Using the same (empty) brush, work quickly over the
surface again in the same direction(s) to distribute the glaze
as evenly as possible. Allow to dry (2–3 hours).

Notes If planning your own project, protect with a sealant
for a hardwearing finish (see pages 42–3).

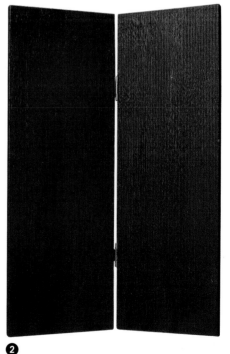

❶ DARK GREEN
The basic recipe
is brushed over
a medium green
base coat of

3½tbsp white latex
flat, plus 2tbsp
monestial green
and 4tsp medium
gray acylics.

❷ DARK RED
Here I added 1tbsp
cadmium red and
2tsp burnt umber
acrylics to the

glazing liquid.
For the base coat
I used a premixed
deep red latex flat.

WATER-BASED CRACKLE

This traditional form of paint distressing simulates the attractive crazing that appears on painted wooden surfaces subjected to temperature changes and will disguise even the ugliest plastic laminate. Originally undertaken only with oil-based materials, this technique used to produce unpredictable results. Fortunately, the water-based version is far easier to use. It is wise, however, to choose premixed latex paint and work on a warm, dry (but not hot) day. Color choice is important—use contrasting colors for a bold effect, closer tones for a subtler look.

BASIC RECIPE—GREEN ON BLUE

MATERIALS
Quantities for Wardrobe Shelving (see page 60)
Base coat ▶ 25 fl. oz. (740ml.) premixed bright blue latex flat paint
Crackle coat ▶ 20 fl. oz. (600ml.) acrylic crackle varnish (transparent)
Top coat ▶ 25 fl. oz. (740ml.) premixed bright green latex flat paint

EQUIPMENT
Mixing sticks / 2 x 2in. (50mm.) latex brushes / 1 x 1–2in. (25–50mm.) tossaway brush

INSTRUCTIONS
Base coat
Stir the latex paint well, and apply a good, even coat to the prepared and primed surface (see pages 12–17), using one of the latex brushes. Allow to dry (2–3 hours).

Crackle coat
Stir the crackle varnish well, and apply one or two even coats with the tossaway brush. The thickness of the varnish and the direction in which you brush will determine the size and type of cracks. To create relatively few, large cracks, apply two generous coats; one sparing coat will create much smaller cracks and so will one or two well-worked coats. For horizontal cracks, brush the varnish horizontally; for vertical cracks, brush vertically; for a mixture of the two, cross brush, applying one coat vertically and the other horizontally. Allow 1–2 hours for each coat to dry. The cracks appear as the varnish dries and begins to work against the base coat.

Top coat
Stir the latex paint well, brush an even coat onto the varnished surface with the other latex brush, and allow to dry (2–3 hours). The cracks will begin to reappear within approx. 5 minutes. When the top coat is completely dry, the base coat beneath the varnish will be clearly apparent.

Notes If planning your own project, protect with a sealant for a hardwearing finish (see pages 42–3).

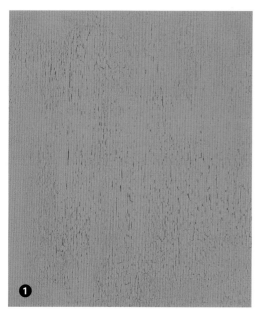

❶ GREEN ON BLUE
The colorway used for the basic recipe; this swatch shows the effects of one sparing coat of vertical brushing.

❷ LIME YELLOW ON PALE PURPLE
Vertical brushing again, but I applied two coats of varnish this time, working them both well. The results are similar, although the fine crazing is more evenly spread.

❸ PALE PINK ON MOSS GREEN
Still more vertical brushing and again two coats of varnish, but now the crazing is negligible and the cracks are broader. Why? I was generous with the varnish but did not overwork it.

❹ PALE PURPLE ON LIME YELLOW
The only example of horizontal brushing. Here again I used two generous coats of varnish to produce broad cracks and just a little crazing.

WATER-BASED DRAGGING

For this technique a long-haired brush is used to draw fine lines through translucent colored glaze to reveal a base coat of a different color. Because it is derived from wood graining, dragging works well on furniture. This version of the traditional oil-based technique has much to recommend it. The use of standard latex brushes instead of specialist dragging brushes certainly cuts costs, as do the less expensive latex paints and/or artists' acrylics used to tint the glaze. Water-based glazes also dry more quickly than oil-based ones, and although this could be a great disadvantage when working on large areas such as walls, it's unlikely to cause problems when painting furniture. In fact, scale works entirely in your favor. You are not going to face the problem of trying to maintain a straight vertical line from ceiling to baseboard!

Color will determine the feel of the piece, and with natural tones on a neutral base coat, you can even create the illusion of pale wood if the glaze appears to be applied in the direction of the "grain."

BASIC RECIPE—BURNT UMBER ON DEEP RED

MATERIALS

Quantities for Country Wardrobe (see page 54)
Base coats ▶ 25 fl. oz. (740ml.) premixed deep red latex flat paint (2 coats)
Glaze coat ▶ 8½ fl. oz. (250ml.) acrylic glazing liquid (transparent)
3⅓ tbsp burnt umber artists' acrylic color

EQUIPMENT

Mixing sticks / 2 x 2in. (50mm.) latex brushes / container for mixing glaze / spare piece of board

INSTRUCTIONS
Base coats

Stir well and apply two coats to the prepared and primed surface (see pages 12–17) with one of the latex brushes, allowing 2–3 hours for each coat to dry.

Glaze coat

1 Pour the glazing liquid into a container, add the color, and stir well.
2 Dip just the tip of the other (dry) latex brush into the glaze, remove any excess paint on the spare board, and draw the brush downward over the painted surface, using long, vertical strokes. You are aiming for a broken-color effect, so a little of the base coat should show through. Avoid pausing mid stroke if you can, and, wherever possible, work in the direction of the natural grain. Allow to dry (2–3 hours).

Notes If planning your own project, protect with a sealant for a hardwearing finish (see pages 42–3).

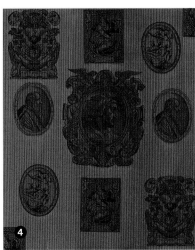

❶ BURNT UMBER ON DEEP RED
The dark-over-light colorway of the basic recipe can work like an aging glaze, suggesting the patina of time.

❷ WHITE ON CREAM
Base coat: 20 fl oz (600ml) white latex flat; acrylics—4 oz (120ml) raw umber, 2tbsp medium gray. Glaze color: 3½tbsp white latex flat.

❸ DARK PURPLE ON PALE PURPLE
Base coat: 25 oz (740ml) white latex flat; acrylic—1½tbsp dioxazine purple. Glaze-coat color: 3½tbsp dioxazine purple.

❹ DARK ORANGE ON LIGHT ORANGE
Base coat: 22 oz (650ml) white latex flat; acrylic—6tbsp cadmium orange. Glaze-coat color: 3½tbsp cadmium orange.

COLORWASHING

Colorwashing—the most familiar of the broken-color techniques and the easiest—is normally associated with walls, but it can be used just as successfully on furniture. The two methods demonstrated give lovely yet differing finishes and would look good in a traditional or modern interior. Once worked only in dark, somber tones, colorwashing is now used with a vast array of colors to great effect.

BASIC RECIPE—DEEP RED ON ORANGE

MATERIALS

Quantities for Rush Chair (see page 100)
Base coats ▶ 1 pint (500ml.) premixed orange latex flat paint (2 coats)
Glaze coat ▶ 8½ fl. oz. (250ml.) acrylic glazing liquid (transparent) / 3½ fl. oz. (100ml.) vermilion artists' acrylic color / 3⅓tbsp. cadmium red artists' acrylic color

EQUIPMENT

Mixing sticks / 2 x 2in. (50mm.) latex brushes / container for glaze

INSTRUCTIONS
Base coats

Stir well and apply two good, even coats to the prepared and primed surface (see pages 12–17), using one of the latex brushes. Allow 2–3 hours for each coat to dry.

❶ DEEP RED ON ORANGE
The basic recipe's hot, modern colorway needs careful placing.

❷ DEEP GREEN ON AQUA BLUE
Base coat: 15 oz (440ml) white latex flat; acrylics—2tbsps cerulean blue and monestial green. Glaze-coat color: acrylics—5tbsps monestial green and cobalt blue.

❸ DARK BLUE ON SOFT GRAY
Base coat: 15 oz (440ml) white latex flat; artists' acrylic —4tbsp medium gray. Glaze-coat color: 3½oz (100ml) Prussian blue, 3⅓tbsp burnt umber.

❹ PALE BLUE ON BLUSH WHITE
Base coat: 15 oz (440ml) white latex flat; artists' acrylics—3tbsp permanent rose, 1tbsp yellow ocher. Glaze-coat color: 3½oz (100ml) cobalt blue, 3⅓tbsp white latex flat.

Glaze coat

1 Pour the glazing liquid into the container, add the colors, and stir well.

2 Dip just the tip—approx. 1in. (2.5cm.)—of the other (dry) latex brush into the glaze, and take off any excess paint on the lip of the container.

3 Apply with random strokes over the entire surface. As in dragging (see page 150), another broken-color effect, you should still be able to see some of the base coat beneath. Highlight areas of detail with slightly increased coverage.

4 Using the same (empty) brush, go quickly over the entire surface again with random brush strokes—your aim now is to add more texture to the surface so the brush strokes remain apparent. Allow to dry (2–3 hours).

Notes If you are planning your own project, protect with a sealant for a hardwearing finish (see pages 42–3).

VARIATION—BRUSHING ON AND OFF

This is essentially another method of colorwashing, rather than a different technique. You apply the glaze with a full brush, aiming for complete, even coverage, and then quickly rework the glaze surface with the same (empty) brush, using random strokes to take off some of the glaze and reveal the base coat beneath.

The final effect is softer and subtler than that of basic colorwashing. You see fewer brush strokes so the paint looks less fussed over or "worked." But because it is more difficult to maintain a consistent texture for large areas, it's probably safer to use the basic recipe for, say, a wardrobe. Brushing on and off will also need protection for a hardwearing finish (see pages 42–3).

❶ PALE YELLOW ON DEEP PINK
Base coat: 12½oz (370ml) white latex flat; acrylic —4 oz (120ml) permanent rose. Glaze-coat color: 5tbsp cadmium yellow.

❷ PURPLE ON LAVENDER
Base coat: 12½oz (370ml) white latex flat; acrylic—4 oz (120ml) dioxazine purple. Glaze-coat color: 4tbsp dioxazine purple.

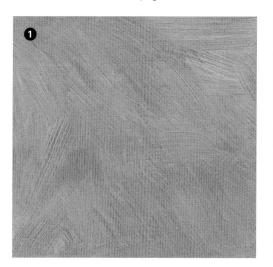

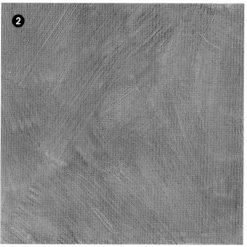

SPATTER ON A TEXTURED BASE

This technique sprang from experiments to create a stone effect with real depth for the Lapis Café Table, and it really combines two in one—sponging (with some stippling on the side), plus spatter. I followed through with the sandstone stool and reckon that with a few color trials, you could turn up a convincing granite, too. But the third stool opposite, took another, more imaginative direction—the combination of bright modern colors on a contrasting ground. All these colorways will probably look best on simple furniture with plain lines, and their busy, textured look might usefully conceal a less-than-perfect surface.

To return to my two-in-one theme, if you cut the spatter coats of the basic recipe entirely, you have an attractive, restful effect that could bring new life to depressing old bedroom furniture. Experiment with soft, harmonizing pastel colors.

BASIC RECIPE—LAPIS LAZULI

MATERIALS

Quantities for Stool (see opposite)
Base coat ▶ 5tbsp. white latex flat paint / 3⅓tbsp. cobalt blue artists' acrylic color
First glaze coat ▶ 3⅓tbsp. acrylic glazing liquid (transparent) / 2½tsp. ultramarine artists' acrylic color / 1tbsp. water
Second and third glaze coats ▶ 3½ fl. oz. (100ml.) acrylic glazing liquid (transparent) / 5tsp. ultramarine artists' acrylic color / 1tsp. Mars black artists' acrylic color / 2tbsp. water
First spatter coat ▶ 1tsp. yellow ocher artists' acrylic color / ½tsp. water
Second spatter coat ▶ 1tsp. titanium white artists' acrylic color / ½tsp. water
Third spatter coat ▶ 1tsp. premixed acrylic gold paint

EQUIPMENT

Container for mixing paint / mixing sticks / 1 x 2in. (50mm.) latex brush / 6 saucers / assorted natural sponges / water for dampening and rinsing sponges / disposable gloves / 2 x ½in. (15mm.) round stippling or stencil brushes / drop cloths / 3 old, stiff-bristled round fitches / large piece of cardboard for testing

INSTRUCTIONS
Base coat

1 Pour the latex into the container, add the color, and stir well.
2 Apply evenly to the prepared, primed surface (see pages 12–17), using the latex brush. Allow to dry (2–3 hours).

First glaze coat

1 Pour the glazing liquid into one of the saucers, add the color, and stir well.
2 Add the water (a little at a time) and stir again. You are aiming for the consistency of light cream.

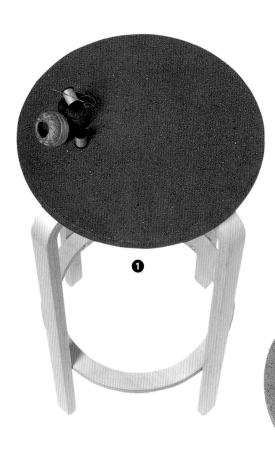

❶ LAPIS LAZULI
The basic recipe: this stone effect can be remarkably convincing given the right context. Small is best for lapis. I sealed all three stools with matte polyurethane varnish 8½ oz ([250ml] for 2 coats).

❷ SANDSTONE
Base coat: 5tbsp white latex flat; artists' acrylic—3½tbsp cadmium orange. Two identical glaze coats, total: 5 oz (150ml) glazing liquid, 2⅔tbsp raw sienna, and 3⅓tbsp water. Spatter-coat colors: 1st coat—1½tsp Payne's gray; 2nd coat—1½tsp Prussian blue.

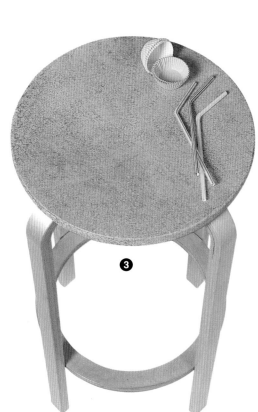

❸ YELLOW AND RED ON LIME
Base coat: 5tbsp white latex flat; artists' acrylic—3½tbsp emerald green. Again, there are two identical glaze coats, with a total of 5tbsp glazing liquid, 2⅔tbsp emerald green, and 3⅓tbsp water. Spatter-coat colors: 1st coat—1½tsp yellow ocher; 2nd coat—1½tsp vermilion.

SPATTER ON A TEXTURED BASE

3 Immerse one of the sponges in water and wring out until only slightly damp. Put on the disposable gloves, and apply the glaze to the entire surface, using gentle, dabbing movements. Reload as required and change your sponge from time to time to create interesting textures. Rinse them in water frequently so they don't clog. It's easy to overdo this stage—remember, your aim is to leave some of the previous coat showing through. Keep the action light, and avoid overloading your sponges. Allow to dry (2 hours).

Second and third glaze coats

1 Pour the glazing liquid into a second saucer, add the color, and stir well.

2 Add the water, stirring again, and set half the resulting glaze aside in another saucer for the third coat.

3 Sponge on the second glaze coat, using the same method.

4 With one of the stippling (or stencil) brushes and a gentle, tapping wrist action, quickly soften the sponge marks. Allow to dry (2 hours).

5 Using the remaining glaze and the other stippling brush, repeat steps 3 and 4. By now you will have created plenty of texture and a translucency which will give the stone effect great depth.

First spatter coat

1 Place the first spatter color in a fourth saucer, and stir in the water (a little at a time). Again, you need the consistency of light cream.

2 Protect the work space with drop cloths before you begin. Wearing the disposable gloves, load one of the fitches with glaze, and stand between 5 and 12in. (13–30cm.) from the surface. Hold the brush in one hand and use the fingers of the other hand to pull back the fitch's bristles, releasing a mist of glaze onto the surface. You are aiming for a series of well-spaced dots of varying size. Confidence is essential, so try the technique out on a large piece of cardboard first— you'll find that the farther you stand from the surface the larger the dots are.

Second and third spatter coats

Using the same method, repeat to apply the second and third spatter colors.

Notes If planning your own project, protect with a sealant for a hardwearing finish (see pages 42–3).

I know stenciling is such a familiar decorator's tool it is beginning to be derided, but simple motifs used with restraint are an appealing, straightforward way to decorate plain furniture. Applied to painted or sprayed surfaces, stenciling can, for example, turn a hideous kitchen cabinet into an object of desire—or at least into something you can bear to look at until your budget allows for bigger changes! A flat surface is all you need. Use flat color backgrounds, as I do here, or experiment with colorwashing (see page 152), sponging (see page 154), or woodwashing on previously unpainted wood (see page 140).

You can opt for speed with spray paint or go the traditional route with stencil or stippling brush. Naturally the results differ—spray can create even, uniform coverage, stippling will always produce a more textured look, and it takes some practice to achieve subtle shading with a spray can. Substitute fabric paints for artists' acrylics, and you can stipple on fabric too—an idea for deckchairs, perhaps? (See page 170.)

BASIC RECIPE—SPRAYING A TWO-TONE DAISY

MATERIALS

Quantity for 11½ x 11½ft. (3.5 x 3.5m.)
Using the stencils ► 5 fl. oz. (150ml.) rose pink acrylic spray paint / 5 fl. oz. (150ml.) burgundy acrylic spray paint

EQUIPMENT

Photocopier / stencil paper of required size / masking tape / cutting mat / X-Acto knife / newspaper for masking / lint-free cotton rags / drop cloths / protective mask

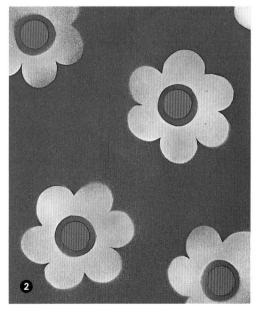

❶ PINK AND BURGUNDY ON CREAM
The basic recipe: the strong color contrasts and dense coverage create a bold, simple motif.
Base coat: 13½oz (400ml) pale yellow acrylic spray.

❷ TWO PINKS ON PRUSSIAN GREEN
The softer look of the petals is a matter of technique as well as color. I used less spray and aimed for blush pink highlights with less even coverage.

STENCILING

INSTRUCTIONS

Cutting the stencil

PROTECT YOUR WORK SPACE WITH DROP CLOTHS BEFORE SPRAYING, WORK IN A WELL-VENTILATED AREA, AND WEAR A MASK.

1 Enlarge the two motifs—the daisy and the separate center (see page 186)—to the required size at the same scale, using the photocopier.

2 Center the photocopy of the daisy motif on a sheet of stencil paper of the appropriate size, allowing approx. 4in. (10cm.) all around the image. Secure firmly with masking tape on all four sides. (If you plan to use your stencil for a repeating pattern, cut a square or rectangular piece of stencil paper. It's so much easier to line up and space the motifs.)

3 Using the X-Acto knife and cutting mat, cut out the motif, neatly following the outline of the petals and the central circle. Press firmly through the photocopy and the stencil paper, aiming for a few "clean" strokes. Lots of anxious little cuts make for uneven edges. Retain two of the three pieces— the daisy stencil and the circle cut from the center of the motif.

4 Use the separate photocopied center motif to make the smaller circle stencil in the same way. Throw the cut-out center away to avoid confusion.

5 Attach sheets of newspaper to the sides of both stencils with the masking tape to protect the surrounding painted areas when you spray.

Using the stencils

1 Secure the daisy stencil to the prepared, primed (see pages 12–17), and painted surface, using tabs of masking tape taking off some of the tack first on a clean rag.

2 Position the circular piece of stencil paper cut from the daisy motif so that it masks the middle of the flower.

3 Shake the pale spray can well and carefully apply an even coat into the unmasked area. Use steady, sweeping strokes and hold the can approx. 12in. (30.5cm.) from the surface. Practice on a spare piece of board first. It takes some experience to achieve even coverage. Remove both masks gently and immediately, or they may bond with the surface. Allow to dry (1 hour).

4 Shake the darker spray can well, and, placing the smaller circle stencil so that it masks all but the center of the flower, spray carefully for an even coat. Remove immediately and allow to dry (1 hour).

Notes Positioning the daisy center is easily done by eye, but you need to use register marks where fit is more critical. When working with the Vase stencils (page 58), for example, I matched light pencil marks on the vase shape with key points on the "stripes" stencil.

BASIC RECIPE—STIPPLING A TWO-TONE STAR

MATERIALS

Quantity for 11½ x 11½ft. (3.5 x 3.5m.)
Using the stencil ▶ 7 fl. oz. (210ml.) premixed deep yellow latex flat paint / 1tbsp. titanium white artists' acrylic color

EQUIPMENT

Photocopier / stencil paper of required size / masking tape / cutting mat / X-Acto knife / lint-free cotton rags / container for mixing paint / mixing sticks / 2 saucers / 1 x ½in. (12mm.) stencil brush

INSTRUCTIONS
Cutting the stencil

Follow the method described in Spraying, steps 1–3, to cut the single stencil.

Using the stencil

1 See Spraying, Using the stencils, step 1.

2 For the pale color, mix 5 fl. oz. (150ml.) deep yellow latex flat with the titanium white, stirring well.

3 Pouring a little at a time into one of the saucers, dip the stencil brush into the paint and dab it gently onto the entire unmasked area with a light stippling or tapping wrist action. You should be able to see some of the top coat beneath.

4 Stir the remaining 2 fl. oz. (60ml.) deep yellow latex flat well, and, using the same method and brush, apply the darker color down one side of the motif to sharpen the image.

5 Again using the same (this time empty) brush and action, go quickly over the same areas to soften the meeting of the dark and light tones. Allow to dry (1 hour).

Notes If planning your own project, protect all stencils with a sealant for a hardwearing finish (see pages 42–3).

❶ TWO YELLOWS ON DEEP BLUE
The two-tone stars of the basic recipe are set on a hand-painted base of 1 pint (500ml) deep blue latex flat. The more textured effect of stippling is very apparent. Don't make the stars too small—the paper "bridges" will be vulnerable.

❷ TWO PINKS ON PALE GRAY
Base coat: 14 oz (410ml) white latex flat; artists' acrylic —6tbsp dioxazine purple. Pale pink: 6tbsp white latex flat; artists' acrylic —2tbsps dioxazine purple and raw umber. Dark pink: artists' acrylic— 2tbsp raw umber, 1tsp cadmium red.

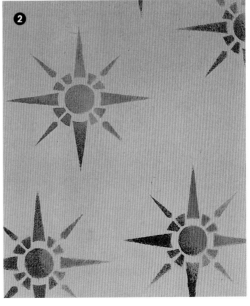

DÉCOUPAGE

Decorating a surface with shapes or illustrations torn from paper is a simple makeover technique. In our projects I've placed small tinted sections formally or randomly, combining them with paint finishes, but you can achieve striking results with total coverage. I've seen sturdy shelves papered with typography, and there's a gorgeous chest of drawers decked with music scores on page 138.

BASIC RECIPE—AGED PAPER ON ANTIQUE WHITE

MATERIALS

Quantity for 38 x 38ft (3.5 x 3.5m.)
Base coat ▶ 7½fl. oz. (220ml.) white latex flat paint / 1 fl. oz. (30ml.) raw umber artists' acrylic color
Preparing the pieces ▶ photocopies as required / 2 teabags / 2tbsp. instant coffee / 10 fl. oz. (300ml.) hot water
Placing the pieces ▶ 2 fl. oz. (60ml.) white glue
Sealant coats (interior use—see also opposite) ▶ 1 pint (500ml.) clear, quick-drying, silk polyurethane varnish (2 coats)

EQUIPMENT

Container for mixing paint / mixing stick / 1 x 2in. (50mm.) latex brush / small artists' brush / 2 cups / newspaper to protect work surface / saucer / 1 x 1in. (25mm.) tossaway brush / lint-free cotton rags / varnish brush

INSTRUCTIONS
Base coat

1 Pour the white latex paint into the container, add the raw umber, and stir well.
2 Apply two coats to the prepared and primed surface (see pages 12–17), allowing 2–3 hours for each coat to dry.

❶ AGED PAPER ON ANTIQUE WHITE This is an extreme example of aging with tea and coffee —it's your choice how far you take it.

Preparing the pieces

1 Using water and the artists' brush, paint a line around each photocopied image to soften the paper fibers. Leave for a minute and then tear along the lines. Allow to dry. You are aiming for irregular, soft edges.
2 Lay the photocopies on the surface and decide on their positions.
3 Put teabags in one cup, coffee in the other. Pour 5 fl. oz. (150ml.) hot water into each cup. Do not stir. Leave to cool.
4 Pour away the tea and wipe the teabags over the photocopies. Allow to dry (1 hour). Keep the teabags.

Placing the pieces

1 Protecting the work surface with newspaper, pour a little white glue into the saucer, and, using the household brush, apply a thin coat to the back of each photocopy.

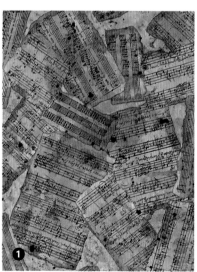

2 Smooth each piece carefully into place with a clean rag, making sure the paper lies flat with no bubbles underneath it. Allow to dry (2 hours).

Further aging

1 Dampening the teabags if necessary, wipe over the entire surface, including the paint.

2 Pour most of the coffee away to leave just the granules and approx. 1 teaspoon of liquid. Dipping the tips of your fingers into the remaining coffee, flick a few granules over the surface (See page 39). Allow to dry (8 hours).

Sealant coats

For interior use, stir the polyurethane varnish well and apply two coats, allowing 3–4 hours for each coat to dry. For exterior use, substitute marine varnish and apply three to four coats, according to the manufacturer's instructions.

TINTING WITH WATER-BASED INKS

❶ AGED PAPER USING SEPIA INK
Base: 1 pint (500ml) matte black paint (2 coats). Tinting: 5 oz (150ml) sepia ink. Glaze: 5 oz (150ml) acrylic glazing liquid plus 3½ oz (100ml) white latex flat; dry brushed. Sealant: see opposite.

❷ YELLOW OCHER ON SHAKER GREEN
Base coat: 3½ oz (100ml) white latex flat; acrylics—4 oz (120ml) Hooker's green, 2tbsp yellow ocher. Glaze: glazing liquid as above, tinted with 3½ oz (100ml) yellow ocher acrylic. Sealant: see opposite.

❸ ORANGE ON DEEP BLUE
Base coat: 8½ oz (250ml) blue latex flat. Glaze: glazing liquid as above, tinted with 3½tbsp cadmium orange acrylic. Sealant: see opposite.

You can create a variety of effects by substituting water-based inks for tea and coffee. Place a little ink in a saucer, using the ink dropper provided. Dilute with water (1 part ink to 20 parts water) and apply to the photocopies with a damp cotton swab. Lightly dab with a dry, clean natural sponge to take up excess ink and eliminate strokes. Your aim is to seal and color (not soak) the pieces. Allow to dry (1 hour). Place as opposite and then dry brush a glaze coat (see captions) and seal.

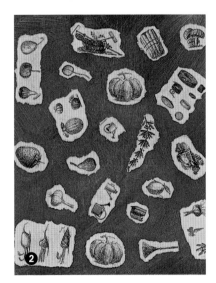

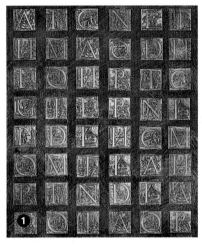

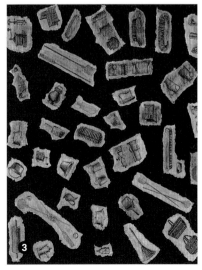

ROLLER PATTERNS

Gingham and tartan effects are easily achieved using seam rollers and are a lively way to customize flat surfaces. Color determines the look, and there's a wide range of patterns to copy or use as inspiration. I've used artists' brushes to paint in narrow grids, varied the grid size, and, on the CD rack on page 104, offset them for more interest.

BASIC RECIPE—MEDIUM AND DEEP BLUE ON TURQUOISE

MATERIALS

Quantities for Gingham Trunk (see page 115)
Base coats ▶ 13½ fl. oz. (400ml.) white latex flat paint / 3½ fl. oz. (100ml.) cerulean blue artists' acrylic color (2 coats)
Rolling the grid ▶ 9½ fl. oz. (280ml.) white latex flat paint / 7 fl. oz. (210ml.) ultramarine blue artists' acrylic color

EQUIPMENT

3 containers for mixing paint / mixing sticks / 1 x 2in (50mm.) latex brush / china markers or soft colored pencils (to match stripes) / ruler or straightedge / right-angled triangle / 2 large plates / 2 x 1in. (25mm.) foam seam rollers / piece of board

INSTRUCTIONS
Base coats

1 Pour the latex paint into one of the containers, add the color, and stir well.
2 Apply two good, even coats to the primed and prepared surface (see pages 12–17) with the latex brush, allowing 2–3 hours for each coat to dry.

Planning

Using the china marker or colored pencil, ruler (or straightedge), and triangle, measure and draw a series of vertical and horizontal lines to create a grid of approx. 3½in. (9cm.) squares on the painted surface. If you are working on a piece with drawers, replace them first so the tartan on them will match. Remove before painting!

Rolling the grid

1 Mix the medium blue in the second container, using 5½ fl. oz. (160ml.) white and 3 fl. oz. (90ml.) ultramarine blue and stirring well.
2 Pour a little at a time onto one of the large plates and flatten with the roller. Cover evenly by pushing the roller steadily through the paint; test on a piece of board.
3 Center the roller on one of the vertical grid lines and roll the paint onto the surface. Reload and, following the grid, roll in the remaining verticals. Allow to dry (1–2 hours).
4 Mix the deep blue, using the rest of the white and blue, and roll in the horizontals. Allow to dry (1–2 hours).

Notes If planning your own project, protect with a sealant for a hardwearing finish (see pages 42–3).

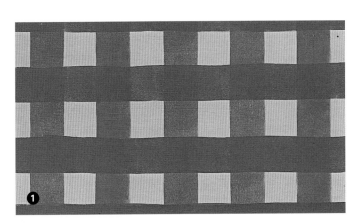

❶ TWO BLUES ON TURQUOISE
The basic recipe: you need to vary pressure and paint quantity to create the crossover look of gingham fabric. Experiment on a spare board first.

❷ RED GINGHAM
This classic colorway is simply achieved, using the same premixed bright red latex flat (1 pint [500ml]) for verticals and horizontals on a base coat of 1 pint (500ml) white latex flat.

❸ SUNNY TARTAN
Base coat: 20 oz (600ml) white latex flat; acrylics —3½ oz (100ml) bright green, 3½tbsp cadmium yellow. 1st grid: 10 oz (300ml) white latex; artists' acrylic —3⅓tbsp pale olive green. 2nd grid: 2tbsp white latex; artists' acrylic —4tbsp cadmium scarlet.

❹ TRAD TARTAN
Base coat: 1 pint (500ml) blue latex flat. 1st grid: 1 pint (500ml) emerald green latex flat. 2nd and 3rd grids: 6tbsps in bright red latex flat and white. Liner 1 follows the 1st grid; liner 2 makes another by bisecting the 1st.

STAMPING

Like stenciling, stamped motifs are an excellent way to decorate a flat painted surface—wood, laminate, or fabric. In their simplest form they can be improvised, like the chic spot design featured on the Stamped Café Table. Try cutting others from the cheapest kind of even-textured household sponge. Store-bought stamps will give a hard-edged, accurate image and are now available in hundreds of designs. Or you can draw your own motifs and ask your local art supply store for details of printers or specialist companies who will make them for you.

BASIC RECIPE—USING ARTISTS' ACRYLICS OR LATEX FLAT

MATERIALS

Quantities for Stamped Café Table—outer circle (see page 86)
Stamping the spots ▶ 4tbsp. titanium white artists' acrylic color / 4tbsp. permanent light blue (phthalocyanine blue) artists' acrylic color

EQUIPMENT

2 saucers / mixing sticks / 2 x 1¼–1½in. (30–40mm.)-diameter sponges for mini-roller

INSTRUCTIONS
Stamping the spots

1 Place the first color (titanium white) in one of the saucers, and use a mixing stick to flatten the paint slightly.
2 Dip the end of one of the dry sponge rollers into the paint and rock it gently from side to side, making sure it is completely covered. Now experiment with your simple stamp on a piece of board, pressing the end onto the surface to make a series of spots. You'll soon find out how much paint and pressure to apply.

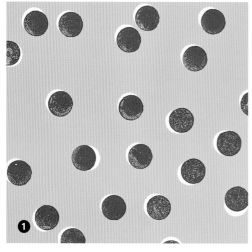

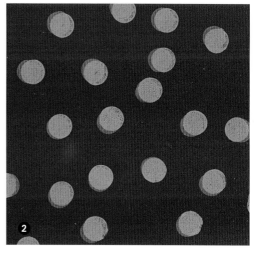

❶ BLUE ON WHITE
This is stamped on a plain yellow latex flat base (10 oz [300ml]). The basic recipe would give a bright, fresh look to kitchen cabinets. This design could be adapted for fabric painting (see page 170).

❷ PINK ON ORANGE
Base: 5 oz (150ml) white latex flat; acrylics—3½ oz (100ml) crimson, 3½tbsp cadmium red.
1st stamp: acrylic— 4tbsp cadmium red.
2nd stamp: acrylics — 2½tbsp permanent rose, 1½tbsp titanium white.

3 Once you feel confident, reload the roller and stamp random spots all over the painted surface. Allow to dry (1 hour).

4 Using the same method and the second sponge roller, stamp the second color on top of the first, positioning it slightly off center. You are aiming for a blue spot with a just perceptible white highlight; the effect will be three dimensional. Allow to dry (1 hour).

Notes If planning your own project, protect with a sealant for a hardwearing finish (see pages 42–3).

USING INK STAMP PADS

The water-based ink stamp pads made for fabric printing are now available in a wide variety of colors and offer the best coverage, shortest drying-time, and a good hardwearing finish for stamping on wood. The simple technique is the same for both surfaces. Push your bought stamp gently but firmly onto the pad, rocking it slightly to ensure complete coverage. Turn it over to check and then press carefully down onto a test piece. Apply and remove equally carefully. Allow to dry (30 minutes).

I used a burgundy fabric stamp pad for the leaf and feather motifs on what had started life as an unpainted but sealed child's play table. The surface was prepared and primed (see pages 12–17) and then painted with a mix of 7 oz (210ml) white latex flat, 2tbsp yellow ocher and 4tsp raw umber (both artists' acrylics). The fabric lampshade was also stamped on a sponged base of 3¹/₂ oz (100ml) acrylic glazing liquid, plus 5tsp dioxazine purple (see page 170, Glaze coat only, for the technique).

METAL EFFECTS

The interest in metal finishes on furniture shows no sign of abating. Ideas on pages 92–3 give you some idea why. These are strong, dramatic effects with the potential to dominate modern or traditional settings—and they cost a fraction of the real thing! My pewter and copper finishes use a metallic spray for the base coat. Recent improvements in quality mean that authenticity is now more easily attainable, but it's careful work at the glaze stage that produces results. Study the real thing if you can before creating the patination. Of course, verdigris—natural weathering on copper and bronze—is the ultimate aged metal effect. My verdigris relies on hand painting, but you should study from actual examples. Because bronze especially was often highly wrought, verdigris is also suited to areas of detail.

BASIC RECIPE—PEWTER

MATERIALS

Quantities for Moorish Canopy (see page 122)
Base coat ▶ 3½ fl. oz. (100ml.) silver spray paint
Glaze coat ▶ 5 fl. oz. (150ml.) acrylic glazing liquid (transparent) / 2tbsp. Payne's gray artists' acrylic color / 2tsp. Mars black artists' acrylic color

EQUIPMENT

Drop cloths / protective mask / container for mixing glaze / large plate / 1 x ½in. (12mm.) round hoghair brush

INSTRUCTIONS
Base coat

PROTECT YOUR WORK SPACE WITH DROP CLOTHS BEFORE SPRAYING, WORK IN A WELL-VENTILATED AREA, AND WEAR A MASK.
Shake the spray can well, and apply an even coat to the prepared and primed surface (see pages 12–17), holding the can approx. 12in. (30.5cm.) from the surface and using steady, sweeping stokes. Allow to dry (1 hour).

Glaze coat

1 Pour the glazing liquid into the container. Add the Payne's gray and Mars black, stirring well.
2 Pouring a little of the glaze at a time onto the large plate, dip the tip of the hoghair brush into the glaze, and dab it onto the surface. Apply lightly in some places, more heavily in others. The plate helps prevent brush overload.
3 Use the same brush to go quickly over the painted surface, stippling or very gently dabbing to take off a little of the glaze. Move your wrist rather than your arm, and work randomly to create the "dirty," mottled look of the aged metal—the glaze should still be heavier in some places than in others. Allow to dry (2–3 hours).

Notes If planning your own project, protect with a sealant for a hardwearing finish (see pages 42–3).

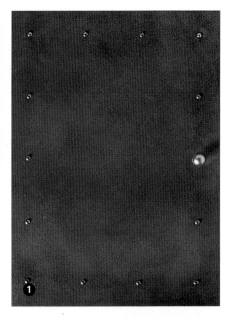

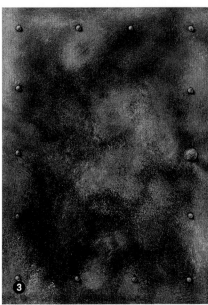

❶ PEWTER
Like copper, this adaptable finish works particularly well in kitchens.

❸ VERDIGRIS
Modify the Pewter Recipe as explained below. Base coats: 8½ oz (250ml) matte black paint (2 coats). Glaze color-mix: acrylics—2½tbsp monestial green, 2½tbsp titanium white.

❷ COPPER
You can create a convincing aged copper effect by substituting the following colors in the Pewter Recipe. Base coat: copper spray paint. Glaze coat color-mix: acrylics —3tbsp Mars black, 2tsp burnt umber.

BASIC RECIPE—VERDIGRIS

There are two essential differences from the Pewter Recipe. First, the base is painted, not sprayed. Using a tossaway brush, apply two coats of well-stirred matte black paint to your prepared and primed surface (see pages 12–17, but remember, there's no need to prime wood), allowing 3–4 hours for each coat to dry. Second, once the glaze has been stippled and before it dries, go over it again with the same brush, distributing the glaze as far as possible to reproduce the "crusty" patination. See above for the glaze color-mix.

GILDING

Gilding is best kept for decorative flourishes—on molding or finials, for example—although it can claim center stage (see the Gilded Table on page 75). Liquid leaf is the easiest to apply, and quality is now high. Imitation (Dutch metal) leaf is cheaper, and the effect is good, but it is more time-consuming. Bronzing powders give a slightly frosted look and again take time. See page 35 for more about materials. Whichever method you use, I think aging adds authenticity.

BASIC RECIPE—AGED GILDING USING METAL LEAF

MATERIALS

Quantities for Gilded Table (see page 75)
Base coat ▶ 12 fl. oz. (350ml.) premixed deep blue latex flat
Size coat ▶ 12 fl. oz. (350ml.) water-based size
Gilding ▶ 40 loose sheets imitation gold (Dutch metal) leaf
Sealant coat ▶ 3 tbsp. transparent polish (clear)

EQUIPMENT

Mixing sticks / 1 x 2in. (50mm.) latex brush / 1 x 1in. (25mm.) flat bristle brush / disposable gloves / soft-bristled brush (optional) / clean dust cloths / lint-free cotton rags (optional)

INSTRUCTIONS
Base coat

Stir well and apply to the prepared and primed surface (see pages 12–17) with the latex brush. Allow to dry (2–3 hours).

Size coat

Again stirring well, apply a thin, even coat to the surface with the flat bristle brush. The more bubbles on the surface, the more uneven your size coat will be, so don't overload your brush. Leave to become clear and tacky (15–20 minutes).

Gilding

1 Arrange your work space, placing the metal leaf close at hand.
2 Wearing the disposable gloves, carefully lift each leaf and lay it on the surface. Your aim is to cover most of the base coat, allowing a little to show through where natural aging might occur —on raised details and at edges and corners, for example.
3 Smooth the surface carefully with the soft-bristled brush or clean dust cloth (see page 35), working leaf gently into crevices and detail, and remove any excess leaf.

Sealant coat

Using a clean dust cloth, rub the polish carefully onto the gilded surface with a circular motion. Allow to set (15 minutes), and very, very gently buff up with another clean dust cloth.

Notes You can distress for further aging before or after sealing by rubbing carefully with steel wool and denatured alcohol. Allow to dry (1 hour). Or create aging glazes tinted with acrylic color to complement the base coat and medium gray to darken (see caption 2). Brush on after sealing; remove excess with cotton rag.

① LIGHT AGING WITH METAL LEAF Aging is limited to the fine lines circling the finial. Dark base coats work well.

② HEAVY AGING WITH METAL LEAF Base: 11 oz (320ml) white latex flat; acrylic—2tbsp burnt umber. I used fragments of leaf and, after sealing, distressed the surface with steel wool and denatured alcohol. Finally I added an aging glaze, made of 1tsp acrylic glazing liquid and acrylics (½–1tsp cadmium red and ½tsp medium gray).

③ LIQUID LEAF No size is required; paint straight onto base coat—I used 4⅔tbsp gold liquid leaf—and sand to age. Base: 9 oz (270ml) white latex flat; acrylics— 4tbsp raw umber, 2tbsp cadmium red.

④ BRONZE POWDERS ⅓oz (10g) copper bronze powder created this aged effect. See method below. Base coat: 10 oz (300ml) white latex flat; acrylic— 4tbsp emerald green.

VARIATION—USING BRONZE POWDER

ALWAYS WEAR A MASK AND WORK IN A WELL-VENTILATED AREA.

Choose a complementary base color, and apply the size coat as opposite. Using a flat artists' brush and taking up a little powder at a time, brush sparingly and gently onto the surface. Reload and repeat until the base coat is almost covered, imitating the effects of aging. Carefully remove excess powder with the soft-bristled brush, and apply the sealant with a tossaway brush.

FABRIC PAINTING

❶ WARM YELLOW GRID ON MEDIUM BLUE The basic recipe colorway: a lively fifties retro look.

❷ SKY BLUE GRID ON PALE PINK For this softer version, the glaze was tinted with 2½tbsp permanent rose and 1tbsp titanium white (both artists' acrylic colors). Two shades of aqua and a cerise fabric paint were used for the simple decoration.

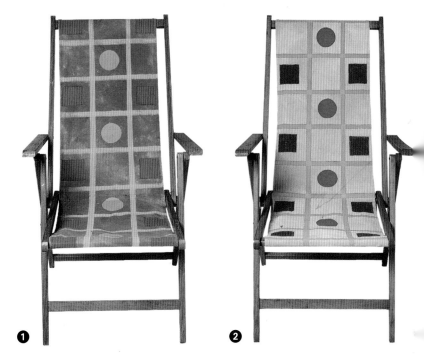

❶ ❷

Personalized fabrics are a fun way to bring originality to classics like the deckchair and the director's chair. Fabric paints and pens are easy to use and give instant results. By combining them with acrylic glazing liquid and latex flat or artists' acrylics, I've created glazes for plain canvas which add greatly to their versatility. Note that strong colors may fade.

BASIC RECIPE—WARM YELLOW GRID ON MEDIUM BLUE

MATERIALS

Quantities for Deckchair (see above)
Glaze coat ▶ 5 fl. oz. (150ml.) acrylic glazing liquid (transparent) / 2tbsp. cobalt blue artists' acrylic color / 1½tbsp. titanium white artists' acrylic color / heavyweight cotton duck (48 x 16in. [122 x 40cm.]—see comment on fabric width below)
Decoration ▶ 5 fl. oz. (150ml.) yellow fabric paint / 3½ fl. oz. (100ml.) peppermint green fabric paint / 3½ fl. oz. (100ml.) orange fabric paint

EQUIPMENT

Container for mixing glaze / mixing stick / natural sponge / saucer / ruler or straightedge / pencil / right-angled triangle / masking tape / lint-free cotton rags / 3 x ½in. (12mm.) round fitches / compass / colored pencils (optional) / iron

INSTRUCTIONS
Glaze coat

1 Pour glazing liquid into the container, add colors; stir well.
2 Soak the sponge in water and wring thoroughly. Pour a little glaze into the saucer, dip the sponge, and apply to the fabric with a circular action. Repeat, aiming for a cloudy effect rather than blocks of color. Allow to dry (1–2 hours).

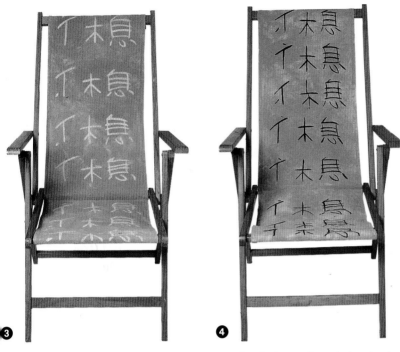

See page 186 for
reference.

❸ JAPAN PURPLE
The acrylic colors
in this pale glaze
were 2tbsp
dioxazine purple
and 4tsp titanium
white. I sketched
the characters in
pencil, applying
lime fabric paint
with a small fitch.
They mean "rest."
See page 186 for
reference.

❹ JAPAN GRAY
Simpler still, here
the glaze color-mix
is 2½tbsp medium
gray and 1tbsp
titanium white;
black fabric paint
for the characters.

Decoration

1 Using the ruler (or straightedge), pencil, and triangle, draw a series of evenly spaced vertical and horizontal lines on the fabric panel to create a grid of squares. Our deck chairs were narrower than the standard size and so was the canvas; my grid was based on a 5¼in. (13.5cm.) square.

2 First removing some of the tack on clean rags, stick a strip of masking tape on either side of each vertical line to create stripes approx. ½in. (12mm.) wide.

3 Paint in the vertical stripes with fabric paint, using one of the fitches and brushing away from the tape to prevent the paint from "bleeding" under it. Remove the tape carefully and allow to dry (1 hour).

4 Create a series of horizontal stripes of the same size and color, using the same method.

5 With the compass and pencil, draw a vertical row of circles in alternate squares down the middle of the fabric panel.

6 Use the second fitch and second fabric color to fill in the circles, carefully concealing the pencil outlines. If a steady hand is not yours to command, it's worth drawing the circles and later the squares with appropriate colored pencils. Allow to dry (1 hour).

7 Working from top to bottom, draw a freehand square in the two outer squares of each empty row so that the pairs of squares and single circles alternate.

8 Using the third fitch and third fabric color, fill in the squares, again concealing the outlines. Allow to dry (1 hour).

9 Carefully press the wrong side of the fabric with a medium-hot iron to seal the paint.

RUSH DYEING

Dyeing rush or basket weave is one of the lesser-known battery of options. But good color and a sound finish are easily attainable, so it's certainly a possibility if deciding the fate of tired old garden-room furniture. I've opted for strong tones with maximum impact, but pastels can be equally successful. Unfinished rush or basket weave is the ideal base, but rare. Don't despair—you'll find all the advice you'll need for working on sealed or prepainted surfaces on pages 12–13 and 16–17. See also the warning about loom chairs on page 106.

BASIC RECIPE—BRIGHT RED

MATERIALS
Quantities for Laundry Basket (see opposite)
Glaze coat ▶ 4 fl. oz. (120ml.) acrylic glazing liquid (transparent) / 11 fl. oz. (320ml.) deep cadmium red artists' acrylic color

EQUIPMENT
Container for mixing glaze / mixing stick / 1 x 3in. (75mm.) tossaway brush / lint-free cotton rags

INSTRUCTIONS
Glaze coat

1 Pour the acrylic glazing liquid into the container, add the acrylic color, and stir well.

2 Brushing in the direction of the weave or rushes, apply the glaze to the entire surface. Take care to work it thoroughly into all the nooks and crannies.

3 With a series of clean rags folded into pads, go quickly over the surface, taking off any excess glaze and again working in the direction of the weave or rush. Allow to dry (3–4 hours).

Notes If planning your own project, protect with a sealant for a hardwearing finish (see pages 42–3).

MAKING THE LAUNDRY BAG

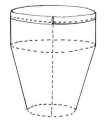

Size and shape requirements will vary. For my basket— approx. 20in. (51cm.) tall with a diameter of 22in. (56cm.)— I used cotton measuring 5ft. x 56in. (1.5m x 140cm.). Whatever the size, the method is the same. You need three newspaper templates: one for the base, one long piece for the sides, and one rectangular piece of the same length for the gathered, upper section. Measure and cut to fit, adding ⅝in. (15mm.) seam allowances all around, plus another 2in. (5cm.) at the top for the drawstring casing. If your basket is flared, the side template will need flared ends. Check the templates for fit before cutting. Machine stitch the upper section to the side and then from top to bottom, then attach the base and make the open-ended casing. Thread with cord.

❶ BRIGHT RED
The colorway of the basic recipe: as for all the other baskets, it was finally sealed with 4oz (120ml) acrylic varnishing wax.

❷ YELLOW
I substituted 11oz (320ml) cadmium yellow acrylic color in the glaze coat to produce this deep, warm tone.

❸ DEEP BLUE
Here I used 11oz (320ml) ultramarine artists' acrylic. Reserve it for small projects because this colour is one of the most expensive.

❹ PURPLE
Dioxazine purple in the standard quantity tinted the basket weave. All four baskets had to be sanded before glazing.

MOSAIC

Mosaic is a great way to transform flat surfaces. With colors as sober or colorful as you like, you can create designs of startling complexity or, as I prefer, total simplicity. There's a vast range of experience to inspire you, either high historical, in the work of the craftsmen of Rome, Islam, Byzantium, or the Italian Renaissance, or in the folk traditions that popularized those amazing skills. My designs rely for their effect on bright color, the combination of whole and broken tiles, and tinted grouts which produce a softly aged look as the wash sits in the crazing. These little doors open up possibilities for transforming vertical surfaces.

BASIC RECIPE—APPLE MOTIF

MATERIALS

Quantities for Apple Door (23 x 23in. [58.5 x 58.5cm.])
Preparation ▶ approx. 160 red tiles / 80 pale to medium green tiles / 30 orange tiles / 20 dark green tiles
Fixing the tiles ▶ 5 fl. oz. (150ml.) ceramic tile adhesive or clear, strong PVA glue
Grouting ▶ 5 fl. oz. (150ml.) ready-mixed white ceramic grout
Tinting the grout ▶ 2tsp. yellow artists' acrylic color / 3½tsp. water

EQUIPMENT

Metal rule / layout paper approx. 17 x 24in. (43 x 61cm.) / ruler or straightedge / pencil / spare piece of chipboard (to required size—see below) / photocopier / scissors / warm soapy water and towel (if required—see below) / 1 x ½in. (12mm.) round fitch (for PVA glue) or spatula (for ceramic adhesive) / tile nippers / protective goggles / box to catch pieces / old sheet / rubber mallet / mixing sticks / grout spreader or filling knife / synthetic sponge / saucer / 1 x 1in. (25mm.) tossaway brush / lint-free cotton rags

❶ APPLE MOTIF
Add a total of 10oz (300ml) deep blue latex flat (2 coats) for the frame, and you have a terrific update for a simple panel door in a kitchen or bathroom. I smashed the tiles in a folded sheet to create the irregular shapes in the motif.

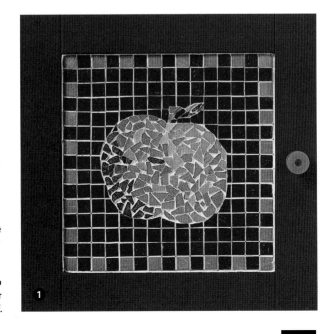

INSTRUCTIONS

Preparation

1 Draw a scale plan on layout paper of the area you wish to decorate, using the metal rule, ruler (or straightedge), and pencil, and secure to a spare piece of chipboard.

2 Enlarge the motif (see page 187) to the required size, using a photocopier. Cut out and use as a template to draw the basic outline on your plan. Set the template aside for later use.

3 Check the approximate positions of the background tiles. If you bought them mounted on backing paper, soak in warm, soapy water and wipe dry with a towel. Work from the outside inward, allowing for the grout between them. The standard spacing is approx. ½₂in. (1mm.), and that's the spacing adopted on the mounted squares of 15 x 15 in which they are sometimes sold. The size or style of a design may require a different allowance, but it is best to keep it uniform. Don't trim tiles, even where the design is to feature broken pieces. Just note where trimming will be necessary. For complex designs I like to keep this rough layout, transferring the tiles as required.

4 Using the template again, draw the basic outline of the motif on the prepared surface (see pages 12–17). This is the time to make small adjustments to its size, if necessary. There is no need to prime under the tiles when working on wood.

Fixing the tiles

1 If using PVA glue and the fitch, apply an even coat to part of the edge of the design—enough for approx. eight tiles. Lay the edge tiles, working from corners if there are any. Use the ruler to keep rows straight. You can, if you prefer, brush the adhesive onto the back of each tile and position (see page 41). If using ceramic adhesive, apply the same method, bedding the tiles into an even layer of adhesive spread with the spatula.

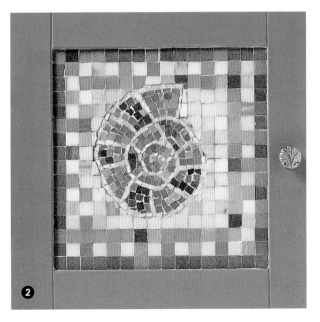

❷ AMMONITE
The regular shapes needed for the fossil were cut with tile nippers. The grout was tinted with 2tsp pale blue artists' acrylic; the color-mix for the two lilac coats on the frame was 8½oz (250ml) white latex flat and 3⅓tbsp dioxazine purple artists' acrylic. See page 187 for the motif.

2 Continue in this way, working inward and on small areas at a time, until you have laid all of the whole background tiles.

3 Using the nippers, trim the remaining background tiles to fit around the motif. Cut with the reverse (ridged) side of the tile facing upward (see page 41). You'll need to press hard and suddenly. Wear protective goggles and work over a box—that way you save small pieces which could be useful for broken-tile sections and prevent shards of glass from falling to the floor.

4 Glue (or bed) the trimmed pieces in position around the motif to complete the background.

5 To create the broken pieces within the motif, use the tile nippers as described above, or, for a more random effect, place tiles of the required color on part of a folded sheet, fold it in half again to cover the tiles, and (wearing the goggles) tap them sharply with the mallet.

6 Working on areas of detail (such as the shading, leaf, and stalk) first, glue (or bed) the broken pieces in place. All your jigsaw puzzle skills are useful here. But remember that there is no "right" way to lay these areas: you are aiming first for an effect that pleases you and second (as far as possible) for uniform spacing between the tiles.

Grouting the tiles

1 Stir the tile grout well and apply to the tiled surface with the spreader (or filling knife), pushing grout firmly into the spaces between the tiles.

2 Remove any excess with the spreader and replace it in the tub. You can use it again.

3 Immerse the sponge in water, wring out until just damp, and carefully wipe the tiles clean. Allow to dry (8 hours).

Tinting the grout

1 Place the acrylic color in a saucer, add the water, and stir well until the wash is the consistency of light cream.

2 Apply to the entire surface, using the tossaway brush.

3 Working quickly with a damp rag, wipe off the excess. Allow to dry (1–2 hours) and buff up with a clean rag.

Notes Prime the surrounding surfaces before you tile, but leave the rest of the painting until the mosaic is completed. You'll need to use masking tape to protect tiled areas. Take some of the tack off on a cloth first or you may disturb the grout when you remove the tape.

Remember that tiles in quantity are heavy and can strain the door hinges. Stronger hinges may be the answer, but don't create whole panels of mosaic on large doors. On solid wooden doors you might opt for a band of mosaic set into routed sections.

Unlike mosaic, punched tin is best kept for vertical surfaces, although I can see it working on a tiny decorative table or, on a larger scale, on something like a blanket box. It needs plain, uncluttered shapes, too, and not just because of the practical difficulties of applying tin to curved or rounded furniture. The Pennsylvania German tradition is the current inspiration for this wonderfully easy technique. These people favored symmetrical designs like snowflakes, tulips, and hearts. Here and on the French Dresser (page 70), I've kept my motifs simple and formal, based largely on straight and curved lines, though the references are sophisticated. If you want to try something more complex, there is an earlier European tradition which favored intricate patterns; I have seen illustrations of elaborate, fifteenth-century lanterns used to guide travelers deep in the Vienna Woods. I'd like to experiment with the Tree of Life motif which crops up in all Indo-European cultures. The traditional material was coke tin —pure tin was too soft and expensive for folk art. Today tin-plated steel is the standard, but zinc is an acceptable substitute. Both need to be rubbed down with abrasive paper for the authentic look of Pennsylvania German work.

BASIC RECIPE—TOPIARY MOTIFS

MATERIALS

Quantities for Four-Paneled Door (see page 178)
Preparation ▶ tin-plated sheet steel or zinc (see below)
Finishing ▶ 3½ fl. oz. (100ml.) paint thinners / 3½ fl. oz. (100ml.) beeswax polish
Securing the tin ▶ 3½ fl. oz. (100ml.) strong-bonding, multipurpose contact adhesive / brass or copper-headed nails

EQUIPMENT

Metal rule / ruler or straightedge / pencil / newspaper for template (if required—see below) / scissors / masking tape / china marker / tinsnips / rubber or wooden mallet / large sheet chipboard (to required size—see page 179) / photocopier / tracing paper approx. 17 x 24in. (43 x 61cm.) / nail set / hammer / cotton gloves / waterproof abrasive paper / lint-free cotton rags / 1 round fitch / bradawl

INSTRUCTIONS
Preparing the tin

1 Measure and cut out the appropriate template(s) for your chosen panels on newspaper, using the metal rule, ruler (or straightedge), and pencil. For our door we needed four rectangles—two 35 x 7½in. (89 x 19cm.) and two 18 x 7½in. (45.75 x 19cm.)—which we drew straight onto the metal; templates are helpful for more complicated shapes.
2 Secure the template(s) on the metal sheet with masking tape, and use the china marker to draw the outlines.

PUNCHED TIN

A transformation for a flush door: for the motifs, see page 187. Note the variation on the upper panels: I punched on either side of the line when creating the pots. Once the metal panels had been glued in place, we added already primed strips of simple pine trim to create four fake door panels, securing them with small copper-headed nails. The prepared and primed door frame was given two base coats of pale green latex flat paint (totaling 1 pint [500ml]), dry brushed with a glaze-mix of 3¹/₂oz (100ml) acrylic glazing liquid and 8¹/₂oz (250ml) deep moss green latex flat and allowed to dry for 2–3 hours. Finally, it was sealed with two coats of matte acrylic varnish. We used zinc instead of tin for this project. To compare the look of tin-plated steel, see page 70.

3 Using the tinsnips, cut out the panel, and then flatten the raised, cut edges by tapping them gently with the rubber (or wooden) mallet.

4 After positioning the panel(s) to check for fit and trimming and flattening where necessary, cover the edges with masking tape to prevent cuts and grazes.

5 Secure the panel(s) to the chipboard, using masking tape across the corners.

6 Using a photocopier, enlarge your chosen motif(s) (see page 187) to the required size.

7 Transfer to the tracing paper. Again using masking tape, position the tracing(s) on the panel(s).

Punching the tin

1 Working from left to right (if right-handed) and top to bottom, place the nail set over one of the lines and strike it gently with the hammer (see page 40). You are aiming to make a clear indentation—not to pierce the metal.

2 Reposition the punch ⅜–¾in. (1–2cm.) below the first hole on the same line and repeat the action. Continue until you have punched in all the lines of the motif(s).

3 Using the same method, punch in the "freehand" holes— the ones within the triangle and circle which form the topiary shapes. It's up to you how you do this—rule guide lines for a neat, formal effect, or create a more spontaneous look with random indentations. Remove the tracing(s).

Finishing

1 Put on the cotton gloves and wear them for the whole of this stage to avoid getting fingerprints on the metal.

2 Turn the metal over and, using the mallet, hammer the dents out gently. This won't affect the look of the design— you are simply flattening the reverse side(s) so that the metal will adhere better when glued.

3 Turn right side up again, and rub with abrasive paper, using a gentle, circular action to create that characteristic rubbed-down look of finished tin.

4 Clean with paint thinner, applied with pads of folded rag.

5 Again using clean rags, quickly rub on a thin, even coat of beeswax polish, leave to set (15 minutes), and buff up with another clean rag.

Securing the tin

1 Following the manufacturer's instructions, use the fitch to apply even coats of contact adhesive onto both the panel(s) and the wood, position, and leave to set.

2 For paneled doors, tap a brass nail gently into all four corners of each panel for added security, preparing the pilot holes with a bradawl. For fake panels, see caption opposite.

FROSTED GLASS

For years the designs available in commercial frosted glass were limited and uninspiring, and it is not surprising that such glass was to be found mainly where privacy was the overriding principle. Manufacturers are now producing more imaginative patterns and etched glass alternatives, but they are frequently expensive. The frosting method described here demonstrates just how easy it is to produce inexpensive frosted effects for yourself. You can color the water-based etch cream with special colorizers, and this adds enormously to the versatility of the technique, making it one that you will certainly want to use beyond the bathroom. It is, unfortunately, not easy to maintain consistency over large areas, so choose simple designs on small projects.

BASIC RECIPE—LEAF MOTIF

MATERIALS

Quantity for Small Door (12½ x 14in. [32 x 36cm.])
Frosting ▶ 5tsp. etch cream

EQUIPMENT

1in. (25mm.) masking tape (for fitted glass) or gaffer tape (for unfitted glass) / scissors / window cleaner / lint-free cotton rags / photocopier / pencil / 1 sheet appliqué transfer film approx. 8½ x 11in. (22 x 28cm.) / X-Acto knife / cutting mat / large plate / 1 x 1in. (25mm.) tossaway brush / 1 x 4in. (100mm.) sponge mini-roller

INSTRUCTIONS
Preparing the glass

1 If the glass is already fitted in the door frame, cover the retaining battens or putty with masking tape to protect them. If working with unfitted glass, cover the edges with strips of gaffer tape to avoid injury.

2 Using window cleaner and clean rag, wipe the glass carefully, taking care not to dampen the tape. Use another clean rag to dry the glass. It must be free of dust and fingerprints.

Masking

1 Enlarge the motif on page 187 to size, using a photocopier.

2 Trace the motif onto the self-adhesive film with the pencil, and carefully cut around the outline of the leaf and its "skeleton," using the X-Acto knife and cutting mat.

3 Peel the backing off the film motif (now without its skeleton) and position on the glass, taking care not to mark it.

Frosting

1 Pour etch cream onto the large plate, and apply a thin, even coat to the entire surface, using the tossaway brush.

2 Working quickly and lightly in all directions, go over the wet surface with the dry sponge roller. Your aim is to get rid of the brush marks so that no lines remain on the surface.

3 Using the tip of the knife, remove the motif and any masking tape quickly and carefully before the varnish begins to dry, or you may lift off some of the frosting. Allow to dry (2–4 hours).

❶ LEAF MOTIF
The basic recipe: the leaf-shaped mask creates the design.

❷ CACTUS
Here the method is reversed. The film surrounding the cut motif protects most of the glass, so it must be large enough to cover the whole panel. Add 1tsp green colorizer before application, and mix well. See page 187 for the motif.

❸ CHECKERS
To achieve this effect rule a grid of 2in (5cm) squares on tracing paper, and lay it under the glass as a guide. Mask alternate squares by applying 2 x 2in (5 x 5cm) pieces of film to the glass before frosting.

❹ FISHES
Follow the method for example 2, but substitute 1tsp blue colorizer. See page 187 for the motif.

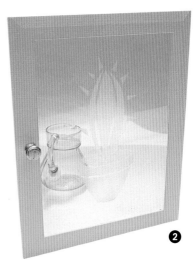

DESIGNING MOTIFS

I used appliqué transfer film for all the designs illustrated above and for the coffee-cup design used on the French Dresser (see page 70). It makes good contact with the glass and therefore prevents the cream from spreading where it is not wanted. For more about the method, see page 31.

Simple, graphic designs work best. Remember that you can achieve either positive or negative effects. The fish illustrated above, for example, could be clear, while the rest of the glass is frosted. In fact, when working with figurative designs, I prefer to frost most of the glass and leave the motif clear.

Notes Use only soapy water to clean frosted glass.

MOTIFS AND TEMPLATES

Here are the motifs and templates used in our projects for you to adapt for your own makeovers. All of them can be enlarged very simply with a photocopier to a size to suit your particular piece. Check the scaled templates before cutting—you may need or want to adjust the shape. We hope you'll be inspired to mix and match the motifs too—the bee or leaf, for example, could make handsome mosaics.

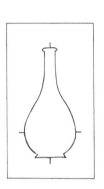

VASE STENCILS Place four small marks on each stencil as shown. Check that they match exactly. Transfer to the painted surface once the basic shape is dry to align the second stencil.

Page 58: Stenciled Set of Drawers

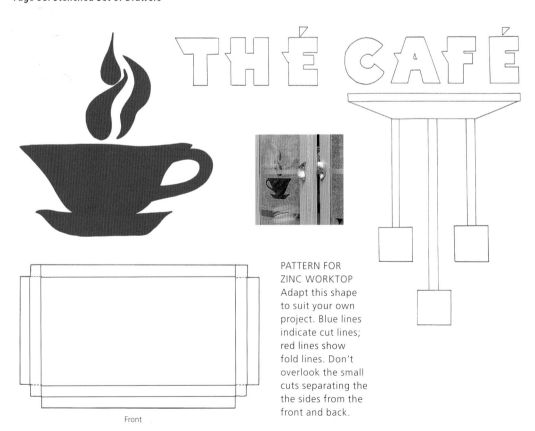

PATTERN FOR ZINC WORKTOP Adapt this shape to suit your own project. Blue lines indicate cut lines; red lines show fold lines. Don't overlook the small cuts separating the the sides from the front and back.

Front

Pages 70–4: French Dresser

Backplate (not in proportion)

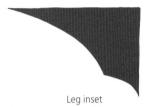

ATTACHING THE BACKPLATE
Note the screw positions. If your table has no base, attach a batten underneath it.

Leg inset

Pages 80–3: Console Tables

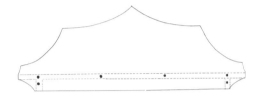

Pages 106–9: Loom Chairs

Page 116: Crustacean Mirror

MOTIFS AND TEMPLATES

Shelf base (not in proportion)

Shelf backplate

Pages 118–21: Decorated Headboard

Canopy front (in proportion)

Tieback backplate (not in proportion)

Canopy side (in proportion)

Pages 122–5: Moorish Canopy

MAKING FLAGS
Cut out the blue sections. You need two stencils to create each flag. Use the illustration as your guide. The top left flag, for example, combines the first stencil in the top two rows. Some stencils are used twice for a second colorway. Position with care.

Pages 128–9: Nautical Banner

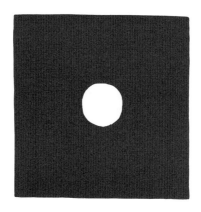

DAISY STENCILS
A two-part stencil plus mask: the method is clearly described in the technique. Just remember to cut out the larger of the two circles carefully and retain.

Pages 157–9: Stenciling

Pages 170–1: Fabric Painting

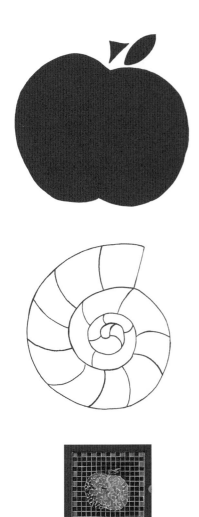

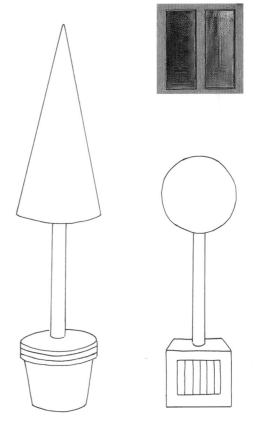

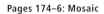

Pages 177–9: Punched Tin

Pages 174–6: Mosaic

Pages 180–1: Frosted Glass

LIST OF SUPPLIERS

Most of the materials and equipment described in this book can be found in art supply stores, hardware stores and home centers. If you have difficulty finding any of the more specialized brushes and materials, consult the list below. A number of the companies listed here offer a mail-order service. However, bear in mind that some suppliers will not send toxic or flammable materials by mail.

✉ indicates that a mail-order/shipping service is available.

Arch ✉
407 Jackson Street
San Francisco, CA 94111
ph: 415 433 2724
Art supplies

The Art Store ✉
7301 West Beverly Boulevard
Los Angeles, CA 90036
ph: 213 933 9284 fx: 213 933 9794
Art supplies

Barclay Leaf Imports, Inc. ✉
21 Wilson Terrace
Elizabeth, NJ 07208
ph: 908 353 5522 fx: 908 353 5525
Gold leaf and gilding supplies

Bay City Paint Company ✉
2279 Market Street
San Francisco, CA 94114
ph: 415 431 4914
Specialty decorating supplies

Carter Sexton ✉
5308 Laurel Canyon Boulevard
North Hollywood, CA 91607
ph: 818 763 5050 fx: 818 763 1034
Art supplies

Charrette Favor Ruhl ✉
main location with other locations
throughout the Northeast
31 Olympia Avenue
Woburn, MA 01888
ph: 800 367 3729 fx: 800 626 7889
Art supplies

Curry's Art Supplies ✉
755 The Queensway E.
Mississauga, Ontario
L4Y 4C5
ph: (905) 272 4460
7 retail locations in Toronto; artist, craft, graphic design supplies

Decra-lead
2601 Portage Road
Portage
Wisconsin 53901
ph: 608 742 8386 fx: 608 742 2549
Supplier of fake leading

Easy Leaf Products ✉
6001 Santa Monica Boulevard
Los Angeles, CA 90038
ph: 213 469 0856 fx: 213 469 0940
Gold and other metal leaf

Guiry's, Inc. ✉
2468 South Colorado Boulevard
Denver, CO 80222
ph: 303 758 8244 fx: 303 756 3545
Art supplies

Janovic/Plaza Inc. ✉
several New York branches;
main office:
30-35 Thomson Avenue
Long Island City, NY 11101
ph: 718 786 4444 fx: 718 361 7288
Specialty decorating supplies, including imported brushes, imitation metal leaf

Johnson Paint Co., Inc. ✉
355 Newbury Street
Boston, MA 02115
ph. 617 536 4838 fx: 617 536 8832
Specialty decorating supplies, including imported brushes

Liberon/Star Supplies ✉
P.O. Box 86
Mendocino, CA 95460
ph: 800 245 5611 for orders,
707 937 0375 fx: 707 877 3566
Specialty decorating supplies, including liming wax

Loew-Cornell, Inc. ✉
563 Chestnut Avenue
Teaneck, NJ 07666
ph: 201 836 7070 fx: 201 836 8110
Imported brushes and accessories

North Star Lumber
16a Dyer Street
Presque Isle ME 04769
ph: 207 764 0301 fx: 207 764 5138
Domestic and exotic woods; specialty items, including moldings

Pearl Paint Co., Inc. ✉
308 Canal Street
New York, NY 10013-2572
ph: 212 431 7932
Art supplies, including imported brushes

Polyvine, Inc.
7340 Greenbush Avenue
North Hollywood, CA 91605
ph:805 259 7673 fx: 805 259 4753
Manufacturers/importers of water-based products, including acrylic varnishing wax; contact for name of nearest supplier

Progress Paint, KCI ✉
201 East Market Street
Louisville, KY 40202
ph: 502 584 0151
Specialty decorating supplies

Reed's Gold Leaf ✉
P.O. Box 160146
Nashville, TN 37216
ph: 615 865 2666 fx: 615 865 1903
Gilding supplies, manuals, and videos

Sam Flax Art Supplies ✉
main New York store:
12 West 20th Street
New York, NY 10011
ph: 212 620 3000
also stores in:
Atlanta, GA ph: 404 352 7200
Orlando, FL ph: 407 898 9785
Art supplies

Sepp Leaf Products, Inc. ✉
381 Park Avenue South
New York, NY 10016
ph: 212 683 2840 fx: 212 725 0308
Decorating supplies, including gilding materials and liming wax

Texas Art Supply ✉
2001 Montrose Boulevard
Houston, TX 77006
ph: 713 526 5221 fx: 713 526 4062
Art supplies

TABLE OF EQUIVALENTS

Both standard and metric measurements are used in this book. Because some equivalents have been rounded up or down for convenience in measuring, it is important to choose either one system or the other and stick to it throughout that recipe.

In following the recipes you may also find the following information useful.

1 cup	=	8 fl. oz.	=	16 tbsp.	=	240 ml.
½ cup	=	4 fl. oz.	=	8 tbsp.	=	120 ml.
¼ cup	=	2 fl. oz.	=	4 tbsp.	=	60 ml.
⅓ cup	=	2⅔ fl. oz.	=	5⅓ tbsp.	=	80 ml.
1 tbsp.	=	½ fl. oz.	=	3 tsp.	=	15 ml.
½ tbsp.	=	¼ fl. oz.	=	1½ tbsp.	=	7.5 ml.
1 tsp.	=	⅙ fl. oz.	=	⅓ tbsp.	=	5 ml.

INDEX

INDEX

ACKNOWLEDGMENTS

AUTHORS' ACKNOWLEDGMENTS

There are so many people we need to thank for their help in the production of this book: Mary Evans, Jane O'Shea, and Rachel Gibson at Quadrille; the valiant Mary Davies, our editor, who certainly now knows her single slot from her crossed head; Eleanor van Zandt for her invaluable help with the preparation of this American edition; Netty, for all her hard work and patience in sometimes tense situations; Kate, Dee, Paul, Simon, and Debs, for stepping into the breach so admirably on many occasions; Debbie Patterson and Nicki Dowey for their wonderful photography–what magicians they are; Alf and Rob at Dimmock Bros.; and lastly our neighbors, who have frequently put up with our turning the communal garden into a workshop.

PICTURE ACKNOWLEDGMENTS

The publishers wish to thank the following photographers and organizations for their kind permission to reproduce the photographs in this book:

6 above Rodney Weidland / Belle / Arcaid; 6 below Dominic Blackmore / Ideal Home / Robert Harding Syndication; 7 Gilles de Chabaneix / stylist: C. de Chabaneix / Marie Claire Idées; 8 above Ray Main / cabinet from David Gill Gallery, London; 8 below Ray Main / contemporary textile artist: Lauren Shanley, Studio 4, Gabriel's Wharf, 56 Upper Ground, London SE1 9PP; 10–11 Geoffry Frosh / Homes and Gardens / Robert Harding Syndication; 46–7 Simon Brown / Interior Archive; 48 Trevor Richards / Homes and Gardens / Robert Harding Syndication; 49 above Henry Wilson / Interior Archive; 49 below Gilles de Chabaneix / stylist: C. de Chabaneix / Marie Claire Idées; 136–7 J.L. Scotto / Agence Top; 138 David Parmiter; 139 above Alexander van Berge / Ouders van Nu; 139 below Richard Bryant / Arcaid.

Special photography was by Debbie Patterson and studio photography by Nicki Dowey. The spray paint illustrations are by Clive Goodyer, and all other illustrations are by Liz Wagstaff.

PROPERTY ACKNOWLEDGMENTS

The publishers also wish to thank the following companies, who kindly lent properties for special photography:

Damask, Mail Order Dept, 7 Sullivan Enterprise Centre, Sullivan Road, London SW6 3DJ, tel. 0171-731 3470; Rayment Wirework, The Forge, Minster, Kent, tel. 01843 821628; Millenium, 1b–d High Street, Barnes, London SW13 9LB, tel. 0181–878 3553, and 12 Abingdon Road, Kensington, London, London W8 6AF, tel. 0171–938 3456.